THE BODIES ON THE BEACH

Sealion, Shingle Street and the Burning Sea Myth of 1940

JAMES HAYWARD

CD41 PUBLISHING
Dereham, Norfolk

First published in Great Britain in 2001 by
CD41 Publishing
1 Spinney Close
Beetley
Dereham
Norfolk NR20 4TB
United Kingdom

jnice@ltmpub.freeserve.co.uk

British Library Cataloguing in Publication Data
A catalogue record for this book is available from the British Library.

ISBN 0-9540549-0-3

Printed and bound in Great Britain by
Barnwell's of Aylsham
Norfolk NR11 6ET

Contents

A selection of speculative headlines on the 'invasion that failed' from 1940.

FOREWORD

At the beginning of September 1940, civilians in the village of Crostwick, a few miles north of Norwich, were surprised by the sudden appearance of an apparently endless convoy of army trucks and ambulances. The vehicles moved very slowly, their drivers sporting grim expressions. One let slip to Mrs Barnes, the wife of a local poultry farmer, that they were carrying the bodies of German soldiers washed up on the Norfolk coast, the grisly aftermath of a failed invasion attempt.

Later that same month Gunner William Robinson, stationed at Herne Bay with 333 Coastal Artillery Battery, was dispatched to Folkstone to take part in a macabre detail. Together with half a dozen other men, he was instructed to search the beach between Hythe and St Mary's Bay for dead Germans. On the first day two such bodies were located, together with seven or eight more over the next two days. All were taken by truck to a field west of New Romney, where they were unloaded behind a canvas screen. An NCO checked the corpses for identity discs and paybooks, which were in turn handed over to an officer. Robinson recognised the dead men as German soldiers, rather than airmen or naval personnel, by their field-grey uniforms. Some appeared to be slightly burned from the waist down, and all seemed to have been in the water for some time. By way of reward for discharging this unpleasant duty Robinson and his colleagues drew a daily ration of 20 Woodbines, and additional daily pay of two shillings.

The bodies kept on coming. On October 21st the corpse of a German anti-tank gunner, Heinrich Poncke, was recovered from the beach at Littlestone-on-Sea. His remains, like the bodies recovered by Gunner Robinson, were removed to New Romney and buried there. Unlike the others, Poncke's arrival was openly reported in the press and by the BBC.

Were these casualties connected to the several long hospital trains observed in Berlin by noted American broadcaster William Shirer? On two consecutive days, September 18th and 19th, the author of the seminal Rise and Fall of the Third Reich saw large numbers of wounded German servicemen being unloaded at the Potsdamer and Charlottenburg yards. His Berlin Diary records: 'I picked up a conversation with a railway workman. He said most of the men taken from the train were suffering from burns. I wondered where so many wounded could have come from, as the armies in the west had stopped fighting three months ago.'

But burned how? According to the New York Times for December 15th, while attempting a cross-Channel invasion of England. According to this report there had been two attempts, and in both instances 'the Nazis were literally consumed by fire. People in the occupied French ports estimate that perhaps as any as 80,000 German troops perished. Hospitals in Occupied France are filled with Nazi soldiers, all of them suffering from severe burns. Thousands of dead Germans have been washed ashore. There was a wave of mutinies in September, many troops declaring they would not face again the "burning sea" when they learned that a third attempt at invasion was being planned.'

Little wonder, therefore, that the chief press censor in Britain, Rear-Admiral George Thomson, was later moved to comment: 'In the whole course of the war there was no story which gave me so much trouble as that of the attempted German invasion, flaming oil on the water and 30,000 burned Germans.'

It is established historical fact that Operation Sealion, the planned German invasion of the British Isles in September 1940, never weighed anchor, and by October had been postponed until the following spring. What, then, was the truth behind the rumours of countless bodies washed ashore along the southern and eastern coasts that autumn? Had a large German force met with disaster in the Channel? Was it really true that the sea had been set on fire?

The myths and legends of summer 1940 are legion, and surprisingly durable. Indeed conjecture that a German raiding force was thwarted by a wall of fire again provoked a national media scramble in 1992, this time focused on the tiny Suffolk fishing hamlet of Shingle Street, north of Felixstowe. The furore resulted in a print and media blitzkrieg, questions raised in the House of Commons, the early release of classified files, and robust denials of a cover-up from the Ministry of Defence. In truth, the Shingle Street story was nothing more than an echo of unavowable black propaganda from 1940, concocted and disseminated by the Directorate of Military Intelligence, MI6 and the Special Operations Executive at a time when Britain's finest hour was fast becoming her darkest.

This study provides the first comprehensive account of the origin, circulation and astonishing longevity of the rumour of the 'invasion that failed' in 1940 and 1992. It is also the story of the ill-starred Petroleum Warfare Department, the rusted death trap fire-ships of Operation Lucid, and the still-secret covert channels by which British intelligence services achieved their first real propaganda victory in Occupied Europe and the United States in 1940. Finally, it is a study of a textbook exercise in the deceptive art of the Big Lie, and of boundless credulity undimmed by the passage of 60 years.

James Hayward
March 2001

FIRE AND WATER

Attempts by the Petroleum Warfare Department and others to 'set the sea on fire' are generally regarded as typical of the hurried improvisations of summer 1940, at a time when invasion was expected any day. In reality the use of incendiary devices, and the notion of combining the disparate elements of fire and water as a weapon of war, is rooted deep in antiquity. In 500 BC the earliest known military manual, The Art of War, by the Chinese writer Sun Tzu Wu, described the use of incendiary arrows, while Thucydides describes how the Spartans used great bellows to project flames. An early flame-thrower, the siphon, was reportedly fixed to the prow of vessels in Ancient Greece, with 200 employed against the Arabs in Sicily during a single expedition in the tenth century. Myth also credits so-called 'Greek Fire' with the preservation of Constantinople through two sieges, and is described by Edward Gibbon in his Decline and Fall of the Roman Empire thus:

> The principal ingredient was naphtha, or liquid bitumen, a light, tenacious and inflammatory oil, which springs from the earth and catches fire as soon as it comes in contact with the air. Instead of being extinguished, it was nourished and quickened by the element of water; and sand, wine or vinegar were the only remedies that could damp the fry of this powerful agent which was employed with equal effect, by sea or land, in battles or in sieges.

By 1200 Greek Fire had fallen from favour with naval tacticians, and its chemical secret lost forever. Thereafter the legend of liquid or maritime fire lay dormant, to resurface periodically like some exotic strain of malaria. Its most celebrated resurrection came in 1588, when Sir Francis Drake launched fire ships against the Spanish Armada off Gravelines, thereby 'singeing the beard of the King of Spain.' The psychology of flame warfare has its roots in an elemental fear common to all mankind. Flame differs from most weapons in that it is visible, whereas the common-or-garden bullet or shrapnel splinter makes its presence known only by its sound, or its impact. According to a War Office appraisal prepared in 1952:

> On the first sight of flame in an attack, the choice of two alternatives, to stand or to run, is vividly presented to a man, and his deep rooted fear of fire, combined with a feeling of helplessness to counter its searching effect, is more likely to induce him to run than would be the case is he were attacked

with normal weapons, whose capabilities and limitations are known... It was at one time contended that the Japanese stood up better to flame than did the Hun, but this was disproved; they liked flame no better than the Germans.

In the twentieth century, the idea of unleashing blazing oil against a seaborne invasion of the British Isles was first mooted by Lord Maurice Hankey in 1914. A key player in the British political establishment, Hankey's interest in flame warfare stemmed from a classical education and Gibbon's Decline and Fall.

Following the outbreak of the Great War, Hankey commissioned a series of experiments by the Oil Burning Committee, a body comprising several leading petroleum experts. Trials were conducted near Sheerness, and on the River Orwell in Suffolk. Although precise details seem not to have survived, his biographer records that initially Hankey succeeded only in burning down a hedge in his garden and polluting a local stream. Though more promising experiments later took place on the Orwell, French fears over possible reprisals meant that the idea was dropped.

The Admiralty also concluded that oil was of little practical use as an offensive weapon, not least because the quantities required were too great, and its transport and delivery too problematic. Undeterred, Hankey continued to ponder several rude mechanicals. On October 9th 1915 his diary records a letter to a Commodore Keyes suggesting that 'submarines should carry barrels of my 'Greek Fire' lashed on, and let it go to burn up lighters etc in the Dardanelles [Gallipoli]...' The prescience of this novel idea will be touched upon later.

Between the wars only the Admiralty maintained an interest in flame warfare, the army having abandoned conventional flame throwers entirely, judging them to be of some 'anti-morale' value, but of little significance as a casualty producer. Despite such scepticism, the dream of firing the sea itself was not entirely extinguished. On May 5th 1937 Colonel Colbeck of the Royal Engineer and Signals Board addressed a memorandum to a Dr Wright of the Admiralty's Department of Scientific Research:

Briefly, the idea is to provide some apparatus which at the selected moment will distribute a film of petroleum over the surface of the water near the beaches through which the Tows must approach. Depending on the amount of petroleum used and, if necessary, continuity of supply from a controlled source, I believe that it would be possible to render beaches quite unapproachable over prolonged periods. Alternatively, wholesale and decisive casualties could be inflicted upon a landing force if they were caught at a really propitious moment.

4

Many methods of providing the petroleum film come easily to mind, ranging from mooring boats with tanks at suitable distances offshore, to laying an underwater pipe line to a suitable distance offshore and turning the petroleum on from a protected tank on the sea front.

Evidently this project aroused a degree of interest, for in December the Director of Armament Development minuted that consideration was being given to the use of burning petrol on water at defended beaches, and in ports and congested anchorages. Although preserved records are incomplete, in August 1938 the War Office informed the Admiralty:

> We are trying to carry out experiments to see to what extent petroleum can be used as a means of defence against landing attacks at beaches, mainly with the idea of keeping a minimum of men actually on the beaches while the bulk are in reserve.

> Our Royal Engineer and Signals Board have already started experimenting in a minor way but have reached the stage where for secrecy and safety reasons they cannot continue work at Christchurch. What they now want is to carry out a small experiment at sea, preferably off Weymouth, for which they require Admiralty co-operation.

In October the War Office requested that Portsmouth give the RESB team their full assistance. Sadly, preserved files record nothing more of the Sappers' exploits, although as we shall see, a series of more or less identical proposals would be more thoroughly investigated following the establishment of the Petroleum Warfare Department in July 1940.

A proposal to attack enemy harbours with burning oil was investigated by the Admiralty off Shoeburyness in May 1939. Seventeen tons of petrol was discharged, and found to burn for five minutes after spreading over an area of 1100 square yards. From this and other experiments, the Admiralty calculated that to fire 10,000 square yards of open water for the same period would require 80 tons of fuel. These discouraging statistics conspired to put the project on hold.

In Britain, the outbreak of war in September 1939 brought about the rejuvenation of countless vivid, ingenious and desperate schemes. On March 13th 1940 the Admiralty circulated a hopeful paper evaluating several methods of firing enemy waterways. The given target was the Rhine in the Ruhr industrial region, and the stated object the destruction of wharves, barges, factories and goods in transit. Three different means of delivery were considered, namely aircraft, fuel-laden barges, and pipelines leading from tanks concealed in French territory. None seemed particularly promising. Air-delivered means, the report found, were entirely impractical, as sufficient oil could not be carried, while the other options underline all too clearly how unlikely the wholesale conquest of Europe by Germany was considered just eight weeks before the unthinkable occurred.

Although flotation seemed the method most likely to succeed,the tactics proposed bordered on farce. Having drifted downstream for anything between 70 and 110 hours, 18,000 tons of oil would be ignited in the target area by air-dropped incendiaries - this colourful finale on condition that the fuel had drifted deep into Germany unnoticed. More revealing in the broader context of petroleum warfare was a footnote attached to the summary:

Any such action might be considered akin to unrestricted aerial bombing. Before using oil, therefore, we should most carefully consider the effect on neutral opinion and possible retaliatory measures by the enemy.

In the event, this unlikely plan was superseded by an existing scheme, Operation Royal Marine, in which fluvial mines were streamed into the Rhine. In the first week following the German assault in May nearly 1700 were released, causing some damage, although this minor Allied victory was swept away in the deluge of defeat. Nonetheless, the notion of floating flammable fuel down the Rhine was not abandoned, and would be resurrected by the US Army as late as 1945. December 1939 also saw the submarine service contribute to the Admiralty's faltering flame warfare programme, a Naval Intelligence Division minute recording that:

The American Navy had been considering for some years the possibility of the Japanese using seaplanes to lay mines, as is now being done by the Germans. They had studied the best method of attack, and had reached the conclusion that neither bombs nor machine gun fire would be really effective. In consequence, they had carried out trials with a small submarine, into one of whose blowing tanks 20 to 30 tons of petrol had been placed. When the wind was on shore and favourable, the submarine blew her petrol tanks, and very shortly afterwards ignited the petrol by port fires or rockets. He assured me that in a very short time a very large area of the sea was on fire, and that it was a physical impossibility to put it out. No seaplane could possibly exist under such conditions.

Evidently some credence was attached to these generous American claims, for the following year similar trials were conducted with submarine L.26, operating from Gosport. The first trial, which took place on April 16th, yielded discouraging results. Diving to periscope depth L.26 blew approximately two tons of petrol from her main ballast tanks, which then spread rapidly on the surface. From this point onward failure was total. Two attempts at firing the slick with the underwater signal gun failed to ignite the fuel. In desperation L.26 then surfaced and tried to ignite the slick (by now over 100 yards long and 20 yards wide) with a bundle of burning rags, again without success.

The second trial, on April 22nd, proved less inglorious. Chief amongst the several modifications were four special incendiary candles manufactured at Woolwich Arsenal, while HMS Dwarf proceeded to sea towing a motley collection of scrap seaplane debris in lieu of a real target. Eighteen tons of petrol were successfully released and ignited, producing a blaze measuring 800 square yards. Further research was abandoned, however, since the blaze was reckoned to be too brief to inflict anything more than superficial damage to metal-skinned seaplanes.

Before moving on to consider the formation of the Petroleum Warfare Department in July 1940, and the various means of roasting the Nazis devised under acute threat of invasion, the legitimacy of these proposals merits brief consideration. For in truth almost all forms of flame and petroleum warfare were in breach of that most ignored of protocols, the rules of war. Due to the appalling human toll inflicted by the 'frightfulness' of chemical warfare during the First World War, incendiary weapons attracted less specific attention in subsequent treaties. While poison gas had accounted for up to five per cent of hospital admissions on the Western Front in 1918, burns and scalds from all causes totalled only a tenth of that figure. Although flamethrowers were specifically outlawed by the Treaty of Versailles, and dropped from most peacetime arsenals, it was not until 1925 that incendiary weapons came under international scrutiny via the Geneva Protocol, itself concerned chiefly with the prohibition of poison gas. Of relevance here, however, is that the 38 signatories, Britain and Germany included, concurred that:

The use in war of asphyxiating, poisonous or other gases, and of all analogous liquids, materials or devices, is justly condemned by the general opinion of the civilized world.

Incendiary devices, held to be 'analogous' with chemical weapons under the Protocol, were therefore proscribed by association alone, a sanction so vague as to negate any practical effect. The League of Nations Disarmament Conference of 1933 might conceivably have gone some way towards resolving these ambiguities. However, the deteriorating political situation in Europe eroded faith in the new treaty, and therefore the inadequate Geneva Protocol of 1925 remained the most powerful restraint on chemical and biological warfare for several decades more.

Flawed as the Protocol was, Britain clearly understood as well as any other power that flame warfare - like gas, and like unrestricted area bombing - amounted at least to an ungentlemanly act, and one which might well prompt retaliation in kind.

'ROASTING THE NAZIS'

Prior to the outbreak of war, the hedge-burning Lord Hankey had retired as Secretary to the Committee of Imperial Defence after 26 years in office. In 1939, with war looming, Neville Chamberlain hurriedly recalled him to Whitehall, and as Minister Without Portfolio Hankey was asked to undertake an unprecedented review of both branches of the secret service, MI5 and MI6. Within the twilight world of military intelligence, Hankey had again become an omnipresent mandarin, and was to play a central role in the creation and spread of a series of potent 'black' propaganda rumours of dead Germans and burning seas which gave Britain its first significant propaganda victory of the Second World War.

In his new role Hankey found himself in frequent contact with Geoffrey Lloyd, the Secretary for Petroleum. The two quickly discovered a common purpose, as Hankey recorded:

> I learned from Mr Geoffrey Lloyd that we had very large quantities of petroleum products. All the oil that would have gone to Norway, Sweden, Denmark, Holland, Belgium and France had been coming to this country and our storage was so full that ships have had to be kept waiting, both at home and abroad, before we could stow their oil. Talking it over together, we came to the conclusion that it was a great pity that some means should not be found for using our surplus oil for defensive purposes.

In May, writing to Sir John Anderson, Hankey advocated a literal scorched earth policy, urging that existing oil stocks should not only be denied to the enemy, but actively used as an obstacle. On dry land, he suggested, petrol stores in wayside garages should be emptied to flood roads as enemy vehicles approached. Concurrently, Lloyd invited the oil companies which made up the Pool Board to consider pitting burning fuel against enemy armour.

Independently, the thriller writer Dennis Wheatley suggested several forms of flame warfare in a 12,000 word paper on Resistance to Invasion, written late in May. Encouraged by his wife, who worked at MI5, Wheatley submitted this highly original document to the War Office. His several recommendations included the removal of signposts, which was soon adopted, and a 230 mile barrier of fishing nets to foul the propellers of German landing craft, which was not. Wheatley also predicted that in the battle to come Britain 'most importantally will be fire', by virtue of:

Fire Ships: The old-fashioned fire ship should be reintroduced. Fair-sized ships should be anchored a mile and a half out, just behind the net barrier, filled with crude oil and connected to the shore by electric wires so that they can be ignited and will burn for several hours.

Spread Flaming Oil: A further development of this is a different type of oil-filled ship which will blow up when detonated from the shore so that the flaming oil will spread over the water and ignite the enemy craft.

Wheatley's paper evidently made waves in Whitehall, for thereafter the author of Black August (see Chapter Seven) spent the greater part of the war as a one-man ideas factory, becoming the only civilian member of the Joint Planning Staff.

Following the fall of France in June, petroleum warfare swiftly become a strategie du jour in certain quarters. That month Lloyd circulated a paper on the 'Use of Oil for Offensive and Defensive Purposes', which summarised possible deployment on land and water. In particular:

There is no doubt that use might be made of burning oil in defence against invading troops. Its use on open beaches is open to doubt owing to such factors as the direction of the wind and the state of the surf. On the other hand, in many places where landings may be effected, there are dykes to the rear of the beach and arrangements could be made to flood them with an oil mixture.

A suggestion has also been made that barrels containing oil mixture and an igniting device might be used with advantage in defiles to roll down a hill at approaching tanks or to be fired electrically as the tanks near the barrels.

Presenting his findings to Hankey on June 12th, Lloyd urged that an experimental programme be undertaken by a small, suitably qualified committee, with technical assistance from the Pool Board. On June 27th, Major Desmond Morton addressed a note to Churchill, who had by then been Prime Minister for six weeks:

Mr Geoffrey Lloyd told me today that he has so much petroleum in the country or held in store in tankers in America that he did not know what to do with it, and was very anxious to try and get some of it used offensively against the enemy. He has collected two or three Sapper officers and had a talk with Professor Lindemann and they are considering ways and means.

Meanwhile, the chief suggestion which appealed to me and which I think you should hear is to use the petroleum in connection with fire ships to be sailed into ports in Germany or under German control. It should not be difficult to lay hands on some old shipping of small tonnage and shallow draft and to fix them up with explosives and a large cargo of oil. If the ships could be sailed into selected enemy ports and there exploded they would scatter burning oil all over the harbour, possibly with most pleasing results. Should not this idea be put up to the Admiralty at an early date?

Churchill demurred until Professor Lindemann, his quixotic scientific adviser, felt ready to deliver an opinion, and in any event considered poison gas more expedient. As we shall see in the following chapter, however, in due course fireships would in fact cross the Channel. In the meantime, Lloyd gathered together a small research team, comprising the Sapper officers from the Army Petroleum Division, and Colonel HE Medlicott, lately of the BEF. In June Medlicott had been transferred to the APD to advise on security at oil installations. He later recalled:

I obtained the services of two young cadets just returned from France and started work at once. It seems farcical now to look back at our plans, but it must be remembered that about one division, and that a Territorial division, stood between the Channel Coast and the City of London.

It is interesting to note that neither of the officer cadets, Sinclair and Henry Hodges, had any relevant know-how. Both were however French speakers, lately returned from a disastrous mission to France organised by MI(R), a sub-section of the Directorate of Military Intelligence concerned with irregular warfare. MI(R) had landed a party of four men near Etaples with the object of rallying the remnants of the BEF, believed still to be at large in France. Churchill later described the mission as a 'silly fiasco', and with good reason: after three weeks not a single BEF straggler had been located, and after their radio was destroyed the party were obliged to steal a boat and row back across the Channel, to be rescued in disarray by the Dungeness Lightship. Whether the two cadets were assigned to the PWD in their capacity as tyro intelligence officers, or simply under a cloud, is unclear.

The first formal conference on flame warfare was held at Deal on June 29th, with Hankey presiding. Along with Lloyd and Medlicott, representatives from the Home Office, Admiralty and Petroleum Board also attended, and agreed that trials at flooding the sea with flammable fuel via 'hulks and barrels' should be conducted at Shoeburyness. On land, the possibilities included tracer-fired fuel drums, and the flooding of roads and defiles from fixed reservoirs. On July 1st the group convened again, and learned from the Petroleum Board that it possessed some hundreds of surplus bulk storage tanks which could be mounted on trucks to create 'mobile land barrages.' It was also agreed that new mixtures should be developed which gave off a minimum of smoke and burned more slowly, and to see through the majority of the scattered independent trials already under way.

Without exception, the crude flame weapons under trial around the country were rough. Few, however, were ready.

In 1917 Colonel FH Livens had devised the fearsome Livens Projector, a large mortar which discharged a drum of liquid phosgene gas over enemy positions, which its inventor had calculated would reduce the cost of killing Germans to just 16 shillings apiece. Livens now turned his hand to adapting the device to launch five-gallon petrol drums, for which field trials at Hythe proved eventful:

> While Livens was explaining how it was intended to deposit these flaming comets upon a beach some 200 yards away, something established contact between two bare wires and the most remarkable display of projection fireworks took place. By a stroke of luck there was faulty connection to the particular battery of drums in the middle of which the party was standing, and the consensus was that it was safer to stand on the drums themselves than anywhere else in the neighbourhood.

Livens' scheme was not pursued, although a Home Guard unit attached to the London Midland and Scottish Railway later constructed a large catapult capable of hurling a four-gallon fuel drum over a short distance.

Concurrently the Royal Navy tested yet another innovative device designed to foil enemy seaplane landings, evidently a priority as far as the Senior Service were concerned. On the Norfolk Broads an RNVR Sub-Lieutenant named Friggens produced the 'Wroxham Roaster', a chain of submerged barrels which the vigilant operator detonated by remote control. While functional, the device was of little practical value, the blaze produced being brief and highly localised.

Prior to the development of effective gelled-fuel weapons such as napalm, the Royal Air Force undertook little research involving flame beyond conventional incendiary bombs. Not that initiative was lacking. Early in June 1940 a Pilot Officer Malders of 13 Squadron submitted his suggestions for 'Flame Throwing

Flame barrage trials at Studland Bay, March 1941. (Donald Banks and IWM)

Aeroplanes' to the Air Ministry. The proposed weapon, tail-mounted and dual purpose, was intended to provide a means of escape for aircraft attacked from behind, and a weapon against ground targets in low level attacks. After some discussion the idea was rejected, it being decided that 'the flame thrower would be a most uneconomic weapon and not be easy or pleasant to handle.' From this point onwards, RAF involvement in flame warfare was largely restricted to Admiralty cooperation, such as the Skua dive bomber scheme examined later in this chapter.

In Britain the development of portable and mechanised flame throwers had lapsed after 1918, and it was not until December 1938 that research began again, when the General Staff formulated a requirement for a tank-mounted projector. Such records of 1914-1918 development as could be unearthed were of little use, and technicians were faced with a blank page. By 1940 June both the Marsden and Harvey man-pack flame throwers had been favourably evaluated, although the later Lifebuoy would eventually come to be widely adopted. Limited numbers of a wheeled Home Guard flame thrower were issued to eager platoons; other devices were of more dubious origin. One, produced by an industrious Home Guard unit in Durham, discharged inflammable dry-cleaning fluid through a stirrup pump. Had such contraptions been trundled into combat, it is not difficult to predict on which side casualties would have been heaviest.

From July 1940 onwards the art of petroleum warfare gained more legitimate standing. After due consideration of several reports, the Deputy Chiefs of Staff Sub-Committee (DCOS) cautiously concluded on July 1st that blazing oil might have some limited military application. It was agreed that the Admiralty should examine the problem with regard to ships and ports, and the War Office regarding land operations and beach defence, and that a final report should be filed no later than July 8th. Given the extreme haste with which both trials and report were to be completed, it is not particularly surprising that Colonel Medlicott's team failed to make much use of the data obtained from similar pre-war trials. Less comprehensible is the fact that neither Medlicott, Lloyd nor anyone else connected with what would shortly become the Petroleum Warfare Department seems to have been aware of the earlier research undertaken by the Admiralty or the Royal Engineers. For as we shall see, it would take the PWD nine more months to perfect their own coastal flame barrage. Whether this was due to secrecy, thoroughness or simple oversight remains unclear.

On July 3rd an interim firework display was staged at Dumpton Gap, a secluded cove near Margate flanked by tall cliffs. Several flame devices were tested, including an exploding steel barrel containing 50 gallons of a petrol/gas oil mixture, a rudimentary road flame trap, two-gallon drums pushed over cliffs, and an old car filled with explosives and cans of petrol, this driven into a dummy tank as it emerged from the sea. The ambitious display was not wholly successful, and only demonstrated the effectiveness of flooding areas of dry land from bulk containers - a system soon adopted as the Static Flame Trap. Although exploding fuel drums also showed promise, it was noted that the other items, 'beyond creating a good deal of consternation amongst the spectators... and exciting some inquisitiveness on the part of enemy aeroplanes', did not get far towards practical application. Indeed the catastrophic fates which befell an attempt to set the sea on fire at Dumpton seemed almost Biblical, the trial proving 'abortive owing to the interruption of the tests by bombing, a heavy thunderstorm, and the receding tide.'

The following day a high-level post-mortem was conducted in London, with Hankey, Lloyd, Medlicott, Thomas and Lindemann among those present. It was agreed that the results of the various experiments justified further development, with the result that Medlicott's team conducted fresh trials at Dungeness on July 6th, again watched from a position of safety by a galaxy of observers, but this time in full - and probably deliberate - view of the enemy occupied Channel coast.

In order to collate the results of the various trials, delivery of the DCOS report was briefly postponed. On the 10th progress was summarised thus:

The great problem is distribution. An oil fire burns so rapidly that in order to produce effective results very large quantities of oil are required... The following is a short summary of other methods which have been examined:

(a) Distribution by aircraft. The quantities which can be carried are so small as to be for all practical purposes useless.

(b) Firing oil on the surface of the water. Distribution by pipe-line or channels from bulk storage on land. By this means the supply can be maintained. If used on inland waterways an effective obstacle could be put up for as long as the oil was kept burning. On the other hand the enemy has only to wait until the fire has burnt out, and meanwhile the smoke might well seriously handicap the defence.

If used at sea only comparatively short stretches of coast could be covered in this way. In either case the installations required would be large and it is doubtful if they would be justified by the degree of success achieved. Where bulk storage already exists close to the coast, as at Portsmouth or in the Thames Estuary, it might be worth installing the means of distributing the oil over the sea in the immediate vicinity.

(c)   An off-shore mine-field of oil drums to be ignited at the critical moment. A large number of oil drums would be required to cover any length of coast and simultaneous ignition is very difficult to arrange. This method is not considered likely to be of any use.

(d)   Fire ships. These are unlikely to be effective against invasion of our shores when enemy shipping may be widely dispersed. A concentrated target is required, such as enemy shipping in harbour just before invasion. A note by Director Combined Operations is attached.

(e)   On land our primary objective has been to devise an effective anti-tank weapon. We have tried igniting oil in tins and drums or sprayed from a tank wagon. The latter method used in conjunction with a road block or defile is promising, though too much must not be expected. In favourable circumstances impressive fires can be produced, but their effect is of course only local and of short duration.

(f)   Various hand weapons are already in production and experiments in their use is proceeding. A portable flame thrower with a range of about 30 yards comes into production this week. An order has been placed for two million A&W [phosphorous] bombs. As an interim measure Molotov Cocktails (a mixture of tar, pitch and petrol) are being made locally all over the country.

In conclusion I do not consider that we have yet got any satisfactory method of burning oil effectively on a grand scale. We can make use of it in various ways to produce powerful local effects. I suggest that the War Office should continue to press on with experiments.

It was already abundantly clear that even the most ingenious flame weapon would be next to useless if not properly integrated into a conventional defensive plan. The task of co-ordinating the various schemes, strategies and fantasies was therefore passed to an entirely new organisation: the Petroleum Warfare Department, or PWD.

Initially the central PWD team comprised the keen band of arsonists under Colonel Medlicott, although early in July a career civil servant,

Sir Donald Banks, assumed the post of Director General. A Great War veteran and winner of the DSO and MC, Banks had in 1934 become the first Director-General of the Post Office, before moving on to the Air Ministry, where by 1938 he was a Permanent Under Secretary. After rejoining the Army in 1939, Banks served with the BEF in France as Deputy Adjutant General, and had risen to the rank of Brigadier by the time he was sidelined into the PWD. The core team was soon joined by a Lieutenant Colonel Pennycook, and three electrical engineers from the Post Office. By the end of 1940 the staff had swollen to 16, with various other personnel posted on temporary assignment from the three armed services, as well as every major commercial oil company - Esso, Agwi, Shell, Shell-Mex and BP, Scottish Oils and Anglo-Iranian included. As a result the Department was relocated to its own offices at Westminster House in Dean Stanley Street.

In 1946 Banks published a colourful history of the PWD as Flame Over Britain. Although selective, and weeded of any detail of the operational use of flame weapons by the navy and the RAF, his witty account catalogues well the multitude of novel incendiary devices with which Britain 'flamed to victory' in 1945. In 1940, however, the PWD's brief was more limited than it later became, and initially extended only to the supply of the petroleum mixtures via a Mixtures Committee, which drew on expert advice from the leading oil companies. The responsibility for developing hardware remained with the individual services, and until June 1942 flame warfare research was split between the PWD and the armament research section of the Ministry of Supply. Initially the PWD conducted its fuel trials at the works of Burt, Boulton and Haywood at Belvedere, near Erith, and then later at Moody Down Farm, near Sutton Scotney in Hampshire, which would remain the principal PWD proving ground for land-based flame weapons.

For these various research teams, the immediate priority was to devise an effective weapon against armour. The fall of France had left anti-tank guns in desperately short supply, with 500 two-pounders and 50 Hotchkiss weapons lost on the road to Dunkirk. Blazing oil would disable a tank not by destroying it, but by starving both engine and crew of oxygen, it being calculated that an engulfing fire might stop a tank in six seconds. Hence flame traps came to consume the bulk of the PWD's energies throughout July and August.

Mobile fuel bowsers were quickly superseded by two more practical measures: the Static Flame Trap, and the Flame Fougasse. The Static Flame Trap was a deceptively simple system, which usually took the form of a sunken road lined with perforated pipes, which were in turn connected to a 600 gallon tank concealed on top of an embankment. The release of the petrol was triggered from a manned observation point, with the force of gravity providing sufficient velocity to spray a 25% petrol and 75% gas-oil mixture over advancing Germans at a temperature at 500 degrees fahrenheit. To cover 60 feet of road required approximately 30 gallons of fuel per minute, and in all some 200 were eventually installed, primarily on routes leading inland from likely landing beaches between Dover and Fowey in Cornwall. At a few sites, such as the long hill leading from Dover to Canterbury, a small power pump enabled a greater area of road to be flooded. No little ingenuity was displayed in camouflaging the feed pipes: across the stone bridge at Kingstone in Devon, the sprays were made to emerge from the gutters, and at other sites resembled handrails.

Flame traps initially provoked fears that the fires raised would wreak havoc across the countryside. The myth was dispelled during tests conducted by XII Corps at a farmhouse near Steyning on August 3rd. As Banks recalled:

> Apart from a door post being badly charred and some blistering of paint, the house was virtually undamaged. An even more spectacular affair was staged in a sunken woodland lane where the flames licked up from the depths... But although one tree trunk was badly damaged, and undergrowth was burned away, there was no general conflagration, and the fire brigade which had turned out in force had disappointment writ large upon their faces.

More numerous, and more useful, was the Livens-designed Flame Fougasse. The Fougasse usually took the form of a 40-gallon drum buried in a suitable location and fitted with guncotton as a propellant charge. When activated, the weapon shot out a fearsome tongue of fire ten feet wide and 30 yards long, and was sited in order to catch enemy vehicles at locations where they would be obliged to slow down, such as corners, hills and road blocks. Dug well into the road bank and camouflaged, the weapon remained safe until the charge was armed. Initially the Fougasse was charged with a mixture of 40% petrol and 60% gas oil, later replaced by an adhesive tar/lime/petrol gel known as 5B. For the most part Fougasses were installed and manned by the Home Guard, and proved so effective that by June 1941 some 7000 flame traps and 12,000 barrels had been deployed, chiefly on roadsides in southern England.

The Flame Fougasse spawned a litter of variants. Essentially the same as the Fougasse proper, the Demi-Gasse was instead sited in the open, and on ignition spread flame over 36 square yards. The Hedge-Hopper took the form of an upended drum with a charge set off-centre beneath it. Hidden and fired behind a convenient hedge or wall, the device could spring ten feet into the air, to descend upon a passing column in a cascade of flame. There was even a Cliff-Hopper for use in certain elevated locations, notably St Margaret's Bay. Should the enemy penetrate inland as far as the suburbs, it was even suggested that lawn sprinklers could be charged with petrol.

Meanwhile Hitler's victorious armies stood poised across the Channel, and while Flame Traps and Fougasses might hamper the invader inland, Britain's best chance still lay in defeating the enemy at sea, or on the beaches. The dream of firing the sea itself was not readily abandoned by Banks, Lloyd and Hankey, and research into means and mixtures continued. Yet it would not be until August 24th that the PWD successfully ignited the sea on the Solent near Titchfield. Pipes from ten Scammel tankers were rigged from the top of a 30 foot cliff and fed down to the sea below the high water mark, producing a combination capable of delivering oil at a rate of 12 tons an hour. Banks:

Admiralty flares and a system of sodium and petrol pellets were used for ignition, and within a few seconds of the pumps being started a wall of flame of such intensity raged up from the sea surface that it was impossible to remain on the edge of the cliff, and the sea itself began to boil.

Surviving footage of later tests clearly show that blazing inshore waters presented no small hazard to the enemy, with any living thing not incinerated equally certain to be asphyxiated by the dense clouds of choking black smoke. Bernard Kimpton, who served as an electrical engineer with the PWD throughout the war, recalled the spectacle thus:

The psychological effect of a flame barrage was tremendous. The smoke was the thing you saw from the sea, with flames shooting out underneath it. I occasionally had to go out in a boat and check for gaps during tests, and I can tell you it was a horrible thing to watch. The combination of fire and water instilled an instantaneous fear.

Indeed the black velvet pall darkening the sky above Titchfield on August 24th did not pass unnoticed. Banks:

It was a glorious calm summer day and the smoke was billowing thousands of feet into a blue sky when 'raiders overhead' was reported from Portsmouth... In any case it was too late for concealment, so the show went on and 'all clear' was duly reported. Next day, however, in the German communique it was stated that South Coast towns had been attacked with excellent results, very large scale fires having been observed in the vicinity of Portsmouth.

Yet here we encounter an enigma. For despite such opportunistic claims, records indicate that Germany had been aware of the true nature of British sea-fire research as early as August 10th. Unsurprisingly, the revelation that Britain might employ burning oil along its coastline much concerned the German High Command, and spurred prompt investigation of countermeasures. German naval historian Peter Schenk records that the Kriegsmarine conducted successful trials at the Chemisch-Physikalischen Versuchsanstalt in Wilhelmshaven on August 18th. Using 100 tons of a petrol-oil mixture, the obvious dangers were demonstrated, for in calm conditions the oil burned for almost 20 minutes and produced a great deal of smoke and heat.

If both sets of records are accurate we are faced with a curious paradox, in that German technicians succeeded in simulating this sinister new defence six days before the PWD achieved any notable success with it. Banks, writing in 1946, and thus constrained by official secrecy, infers that this forewarning was due to 'some inquisitiveness on the part of enemy aeroplanes' overflying Dumpton Gap more than a month before. The truth - a shrewd deception operation - was very different, as we shall see in Chapter Five. Clearly the mere suggestion of flame barrages was of considerable tactical value, for as Schenk records, the search for effective countermeasures caused the enemy considerable logistical headaches:

One early solution involved the use of depth charges, but it was soon discovered that water jets were quite sufficient to counter oil slick fires. Pumping and fire-fighting vessels were deemed necessary to protect the First Wave and in addition 150 (then 200, and finally 800) small fire fighting pumps from the Reichsluftschutzverband (Reich Air Defence Organisation) were earmarked for installation on individual craft of the first wave. The Luftwaffe declined to provide these since they were needed for air defence, but nevertheless tugs requisitioned for Sealion had pumps and fire fighting equipment and these were to be distributed as evenly as possible amongst the assault harbours, mainly for use by the advance detachments.

Further assessment of the extent of the German effort is provided by American historian Walter Ansel in Hitler Confronts England:

> The Kriegsmarine reached a generally negative conclusion about [the danger of] extensive fires off an open coast. A five-mile stretch took a prohibitive amount of oil, boosted by gasoline and fitted with specialised ignition. In isolated localities, such as marshland behind beaches, it was held that oil fires might be made to burn. The Wehrmacht went after this angle as a combat problem, while the Navy pursued the seagoing fire hazard. Both reached workable countermeasures. In the case of the Navy, special fire-fighting tugs, each towing a long chain of logs, were to accompany advance detachments. When an oil slick or burning water was encountered off a beach, the tug was to encircle the danger and enclose it in a log chain. So enclosed, the fire could be towed to sea and extinguished by materials on the tug.

Banks, in Flame Over Britain, suggests that a large order for asbestos suits was placed with a Paris manufacturer, but in doing so confuses propaganda with fact. Equally fictitious is the claim that German trials with an asbestos-clad barge at Fecamp yielded fatal results: Ansell indicates that neither the army or the navy suffered 'noteworthy casualties' during anti-flame trials.

More truthfully, Banks records that the Titchfield triumph also caused 'much excitement' in Whitehall. Consequently it was decided that experimental work on beach flame barrages should continue at Deal, not least because the site afforded the enemy a grandstand view of work in progress. However, the blazing success of August 24th was a qualified one, having taken place on a sheltered stretch of coast in conditions of dead calm. Elsewhere conditions were very different, and the Deal installation, as Banks would later admit, would prove a disaster.

> We drove ahead there against many difficulties. Some of our Sappers were blown up by beach mines. Occasionally we were bombed, and the long range guns from Calais turned their attentions in our direction. The climax came when a north-easter early in January 1941 altered the whole configuration of the shingle, tore up the lines of Admiralty scaffolding to which our pipes had been anchored, and threw back the Sea-Flame Barrage into our laps a mass of twisted ironmongery.

Nonetheless, had Sealion beached at Deal the barrage might have provoked alarm of a different kind. Ignition was effected by a combination of electrical (Phoenix) and chemical (Eel) ignitors, both of which were susceptible to the vagaries of salt water and sand. A simple yet effective solution was eventually suggested by the senior technician, a Mr Zass, who instructed his driver to buy up all available supplies of condoms in the East Kent area, in the process earning the PWD an enviable - if slightly unsavoury - reputation.

By September 1940 the PWD had shifted all coastal flame barrage research to an Experimental School at Studland Bay, near Poole. Another experimental beach flame barrage at Shoeburyness proved a costly failure. Apparently developed under army auspices, details remain obscure, although in July 1941 it was noted that the barrage measured 400 yards long and had taken fully two months to install.

The navy too set up their own experimental establishment. Banks, while vague, indicates that 'various fiery forms of harbour defence and flame bombs' were tested, including laying a trail of flaming oil behind a tanker, and a gigantic wick of coir matting steeped in oil and uncoiled over the stern of a vessel on the River Clyde. The ill-fated fireship operation code-named Lucid is examined in detail in the following chapter. Elsewhere, certain areas of sea between Beachy Head and Weymouth were to be flooded with fuel from existing bulk storage facilities, and ignited by air-dropped incendiaries as the invasion grounded. The latter task was assigned to Pilot Officer DH Clarke, flying a Blackburn Skua dive bomber from Gosport. By way of training, Clarke was allowed just one practise ignition, diving to release his bombs at 1500 feet. Clarke later recalled that:

> The sea erupted with an unheard woomph! which made the aircraft quiver. Almost instantaneously visibility was cut to zero by a black cloud of oily smoke which stunk like hell. Anyone afloat in that inferno would certainly have recognised the similarity.

Flying at low-level from east to west, Clarke was to light all points at the critical moment, then escape under cover of the smoke pall, while his rear gunner let fly at any surviving invaders. In all probability the plan was an application of a scheme first mooted in the DCOS report of July 10th. Certainly it involved death or glory: by September 1940 the cumbersome and obsolete Skua had been largely relegated to the role of target-tug. Nevertheless on the evening of September 7th, at the height of the celebrated 'Cromwell' invasion alarm, Clarke was hauled from a local cinema and scrambled west towards Littlehampton, then hurriedly recalled. Before turning back, Clarke stared out across the grey evening waters of the

Channel for signs of the enemy invasion fleet, but saw nothing.

For the PWD Experimental School at Studland Bay success was slow in coming, as Banks regretfully recorded:

At Studland there were other reverses. The sea temperature as the winter came on was no longer what it had been in the Solent in August, and ignition gave many headaches. The climax came on December 20th, 1940 - Black Friday in the annals of the PWD. That day [Generals] Alexander and Montgomery... came to witness the sea-fire spectacle. The climactic conditions were at their worst. and the brisk onshore wind, though just not strong enough in the naval view to prevent a landing, was whipping up the sea in a line of surf breaking just over our oil-points. Though some of the oil pools ignited, they broke up rapidly into errant fractions which had nothing of the formidable qualities of the complete barrage, and in many cases were extinguished by the surf.

The answer, apparently supplied by Alexander himself, lay in installing the emission points immediately above the high water mark. Nevertheless, the system would not be perfected until the following year. In the meantime, on February 3rd 1941 the Chiefs of Staff Committee, in consideration of Oil Warfare, were informed that:

Beach Defence is [the one PWD item] which requires a policy decision as soon as is possible... Flame Barrages of two types can now be produced with considerable effect, ie on the sea and on the beach.

It will provide efficient static defence, but like other static obstacles it will have to be sited in conjunction with [other weapons] and cannot be relied upon alone for the defence of long beach frontages. Its disadvantage will be the size of installation required in relation to frontage covered.

The PWD have sufficient material for about 20 miles of flame barrage which might be invaluable for certain vital beaches between say Suffolk and Sussex. But if this weapon is to be adopted it will take some time to install, and the sooner the decision is made the better.

A further flame barrage demonstration was staged for General Alexander on February 8th. Senior Staff opinion was finally swayed a month later on March 9th, as Banks records:

Alexander, not content with the ordinary demonstration, asked to see it at dawn when he could judge the actual conditions in which an invasion assault might be expected. The first light-up was in darkness and the illumination was staggering. Ten miles away in the streets of Bournemouth the air raid wardens told us that they could read a newspaper and the Commander-in-Chief was satisfied that, whatever else was the result, the instantaneous transformation from darkness to daylight would reverse conditions drastically in favour of the defence.

With hindsight, it is easy to dismiss as high folly the decision to continue with flame barrage research five months after the cancellation of Sealion, yet the fear lingered that Hitler might seize a second chance of invasion in the spring of 1941. On the strength of the belated success at Studland, therefore, the Chiefs of Staff approved the installation of 50 miles of barrage, the respective allotment to each regional command being 25 miles (South Eastern), 15 (Eastern), and 10 (Southern). With materials (eg steel) and labour in short supply, however, progress was slow, and the original figure of 50 miles was successively reduced to 30, then 15, and finally under ten. The only complete stretches to be installed were at Deal (between Kingsdown and Sandwich), St Margaret's Bay, the Shakespeare Cliff (near the Dover railway tunnel), Rye marshes, and Studland Bay itself. Of the Dover installation Bernard Kimpton recalled:

This was the most spectacular of all, as we had the height, and troops behind that. There were fears that the tests would crack the concrete on the Admiralty Pier, but the heat went out to sea. There were other problems as the cliff kept crumbling and we had to keep sheering pieces off the pipes, or else divert them. Later on in the war Churchill and General Patton came down to watch a demonstration. Patton looked mightily impressed, and remarked, 'That'll burn the bastards!'

At Porthcurno in Cornwall, where the vital transatlantic telephone cables came ashore, a small gravity-fed section was installed to guard against German commando strikes. However, planned stretches in Scotland at Wick and Thurso, and in South Wales, were never completed.

A full and final analysis of the worth of the flame barrages was prepared by General Brooke in July 1941. Yet even by the time the first was complete, the German invasion of the Soviet Union in June 1941 had nullified the threat of a cross-Channel assault. Subsequent trials were instead staged for the benefit of visiting dignitaries and bored Home Defence units. Deprived of a tangible enemy, the PWD turned their energies towards conventional flame-throwing research and the development of smokeless and thickened fuels. Later still came their most useful work in the form of FIDO and PLUTO, being respectively fog dispersal and cross-Channel pipeline projects. The true face of the organisation which many had came to accept as the Public Works Department was first revealed to the public in August 1944, via press coverage of the work of Crocodile tank units in Normandy. Slowly the sea fire spectacle faded from memory. Towards the end of the war Royal Engineer demolition parties were assigned the unenviable task of dismantling and draining the rusting bulk containers. The feed pipes, frequently left in situ, continued to provide scrap metal dealers with a useful source of revenue for 20 years.

The ultimate value of much of the early research carried out by the PWD was summed up by Field Marshal Alexander in his foreword to Flame Over Britain:

These were schemes, bold and imaginative to the highest degree, which were destined never to come into operation. But they, nevertheless, played an important part in the summer and autumn of 1940, not least in the effect they had on the minds of the German commanders and troops. The stories which were allowed to spread on the Continent, and the reports of strange sights seen by German pilots on reconnaissance, were calculated to daunt the stoutest heart among the victorious soldiery assembled on the shores facing England. Besides the known dangers of earth, water and air, they were now threatened by the unknown horrors of the Fourth Element: fire on the cliffs and fire even on the very sea.

Calculated the rumours undoubtedly were, as we shall see in Chapters Five and Six. But what, meanwhile, of the Admiralty's daring fireship scheme?

OPERATION LUCID

Following Desmond Morton's enthusiastic memorandum to Churchill on June 27th, the viability of the proposal to attack enemy harbours with fireships was addressed seriously for the first time in July. An annex attached to the Deputy Chiefs of Staff report of July 10th predicted:

> The use of oil against craft in a harbour necessitates the use of large quantities of oil: 7000-8000 tons is about the minimum that is likely to achieve results. The difficulty of sending a fire ship to a harbour is similar to that of sending in a block ship. An operation of this kind is not easy.

> To be successful an attack of this kind must be carried out during dark hours otherwise she is likely to be sunk by aircraft. The harbour would need to be near the sea and the ship patrols would have to be avoided. In these circumstances the chances of using oil are confined to ports such as Ostend, Calais and Boulogne. And when the operation is carried out the tide would have to be making...

> The chances of passing the patrols that may be expected are small and one torpedo would stop the attack. Similarly the chances of getting into the harbour are slender when past experience is recollected with ships far handier than a 7000 ton tanker. It is for decision whether these chances justify the loss of the tanker or whether several small 1000 ton tankers might be used for this purpose.

Evidently the decision made was affirmative, for early in August the Thames oil tanker Suffolk was loaded with 50 tons of fuel and blown up in shallow water off Maplin Sands. According to Banks in Flame Over Britain, a considerable fire was produced, extending at its maximum to an area 40 by 140 yards, thus serving as a dry run for what would shortly become Operation Lucifer, and finally Operation Lucid. An audacious yet deceptively simple plan, Lucid was envisaged as a contemporary sequel to the fire ships launched against the Spanish Armada by Sir Francis Drake four centuries earlier. Under cover of darkness several aged tankers, their holds filled with a highly combustible fuel mixture, would shape course across the Channel for the enemy invasion ports of Dunkirk, Calais and Boulogne. At the entrance to each of the target harbours the tankers would be abandoned by their skeleton crews and detonated, the flood tide carrying in the blazing fuel to wreak havoc amongst the wharves and landing barges.

Given Operation Lucid's illustrious ancestry, it was fitting that another bona fide naval hero, Captain Augustus Agar VC, was given command. In 1919 Agar had lead the daring motor torpedo boat raid on the Russian fleet anchored at Krondstadt during the Allied anti-Bolshevik intervention. Had Lucid achieved its purpose two decades later, Agar's fire ship operation might well have taken as prominent a place in the annals of naval history. In reality, Lucid would prove an abject failure. Nevertheless, in his autobiography Footprints in the Sea, published in 1959, Agar included a detailed account of this remarkable operation. Although there exist several discrepancies between Agar's published version and the facts as set out in official records declassified in 1972, none tend to suggest that the operational history of Lucid differed significantly from the account which follows.

Having been assigned to the fireship project late in August 1940, Agar expected the Ministry of Shipping to allot him several 'small and handy' tankers, each capable of 15 knots. With serviceable tankers in short supply, Lucid was instead given four highly unreliable tramp oilers: War Nawab, War Nizam, Mytilus and Oakfield. Each drew more than 30 feet of water and had been laid up for several years, and from the outset the chances of coaxing them across the Channel appeared doubtful, even under tow.

Agar, an optimist, elected to press ahead. Early in September the naval dockyards at Plymouth, Portsmouth and Chatham were each allotted one oiler for hurried engine and boiler overhauls. In the time available the repairs were inadequate, as Agar records:

Every effort was made to obtain the quickest preparation for the expedition. One ship was taken in hand in the dockyard on September 15th, after having been in disuse for a considerable time. She had to be docked and scraped, and as soon as she was scraped repairs had to be made to her bottom. The engines and boilers worked all right, but the age of the ship rendered it impossible to produce more than six knots. Another ship taken in hand at a different dockyard only reached the dockyard four days before the operation.

With invasion expected daily, delay was not an option. Working flat out, the tankers were made ready in just one week, and with secrecy at a premium rumours allowed to spread that they were to be used as blockships. The operational plan was finalised by the Admiralty simultaneously with the repairs. With Dover out of bounds to most shipping as too hazardous, the Lucid force would instead sail from Sheerness, escorted by destroyers and minesweepers drawn from Nore Command. Bomber Command would also strike at the target ports shortly before the fireships were due to arrive. Each Lucid crew numbered a dozen or so volunteers, lured by the promise (later broken) of extra pay. Once the time-fuses were set, the men were to make good their escape in motor launches. It smacked of a suicide mission.

A further week was required for loading each tanker with between 2-3000 tons of 'Agar's Special Mixture', a lethal concoction prepared by the PWD comprising 50% heavy fuel oil, 25% diesel oil, and 25% petrol. Bundles of loose cordite were added to nourish the flames, and depth charges and gun cotton placed in the holds for added explosive effect. Thus charged, it was reckoned each tanker packed sufficient punch to disable its allotted target harbour. Unsurprisingly, onboard smoking was subject to strict controls. Agar:

We did so by adopting the old tanker rule by which every match, after use, had to be put back in the box and never thrown away. Besides this, two special places only were set aside for smoking. The matchbox rule soon became a habit which it was to the interest of each member of the crew to enforce.

From the outset, certain senior figures at the Admiralty viewed Lucid with ill-concealed scepticism, notably the First Sea Lord, Admiral Pound. Although Churchill certainly knew of the plan from its inception, it was not until September 18th that he demanded specific 'Action This Day', requesting of Ismay:

Make enquiries whether there is no way in which a sheet of flaming oil cannot be spread over one or more of the invasion harbours. This is no more than the old fire ship story with modern improvements that was tried at Dunkirk in the days of the Armada. The Admiralty can surely think of something.

Since Morton had informed the Prime Minister of the fireship proposal three months earlier, this eleventh hour fillip was no doubt a light torpedo directed at Pound and other doubters.

The choice of target ports was limited by the length of passage from the available home ports and the accessibility of enemy shipping, while meteorological and tidal factors served to restrict sailings to a few days in each lunar month. The earliest suitable date on which the fire ships would be fit for use was identified as the night of September 25th/26th. Shortly before Lucid sailed, Agar was summoned to Downing Street to give Churchill a personal briefing, raising a chuckle when he referred to Lucid as 'roasting the Nazis'. Agar:

> I explained the difficulties and also my doubts about getting the old oilers across the Channel. He understood but said there was no time to change that now, and if we went, it must be 'at once'. He then went on to talk about the chances of invasion, and I remember so well his saying, 'It is not so much I don't want them to come. Nobody does. I want them to be beaten before they come, Agar. I don't want one single German soldier to set foot on English soil.'

In parting, Churchill advised Agar not to hesitate in aborting the operation if the task of coaxing the weary oilers across the Channel became too hopeless. Indeed only the perceived urgency of launching an attack on the enemy barge concentrations justified ordering Lucid to sea without further repairs to its 'cranky' oilers. In the event, just three tankers were ready in time for the first sailing, the force being further disadvantaged by having to sail from separate ports. War Nizam and Oakfield, assigned to Calais, set out from Sheerness, while War Nawab, assigned to Boulogne, sailed from Portsmouth. A diversionary bombardment was also ordered against Ostend.

The Sheerness flotilla set sail late in the afternoon of the 25th, Agar directing the operation from the bridge of the escort destroyer Campbell. However Lucid's first shining was damned from the outset. A strong wind and unfavourable weather soon forced the MTB escort to turn back, and as darkness fell the 'very dicky' Oakfield was also forced drop out. The War Nizam plodded stoicly on, although before long a red glow from her funnel indicated boiler problems. Since the success of Lucid was wholly dependent upon surprise, to squander the 'new' weapon by deploying a single doubtful ship in unfavourable conditions was deemed inexpedient. With great reluctance, Agar was obliged to call off the operation at 10.30 pm.

By the time the signal reached War Nawab the ship lay just seven miles off Boulogne, her crew observing the havoc being wreaked by Bomber Command. Their uncomfortable return journey was later recalled by her captain, Lieutenant Commander William Fell:

> By that time there was big trouble in the engine room, which was common to the boiler room. The coffer-dams between the fuel tanks and engine and boiler room bulkheads had filled with light petrol, which was now squirting through rivet holes into the engine and boiler rooms, where it vapourised. The

two men below passed out with the fumes. The Stoker Petty Officer and another Stoker kept the steam for another 20 minutes while we hauled up the other two, who were unconscious and vomiting badly.

With the highly-volatile mixture leaking dangerously, Fell was obliged to shut off steam. War Nawab finally crept into Sheerness the following morning, the harbourmaster concluding when he boarded that her reeling crew were blind drunk.

Despite this inauspicious failure the Admiralty granted Agar permission to try again. After a more diligent overhaul of the ships' boilers, Agar was able to inform Churchill that four ships capable of nine knots would be available by October 2nd. However, although three tankers sailed from Sheerness on the night of October 3rd/4th, Mytilus quickly developed a heavy list, and the force was quickly recalled by Admiral Drax owing to adverse weather conditions. A third attempt on the night of the 4th/5th was scheduled, this time taking only two fireships for the shorter run to Calais and Dunkirk. But again the operation was cancelled, this time because the weather grounded the RAF diversion.

Continued bad weather, the necessity for further repairs and the need to rest the crews all conspired to delay another sailing. The fourth and last Lucid attempt shaped course on the night of the October 7th/8th, again comprising just War Nizam and Oakfield. However, disaster struck mid-Channel when the destroyer Hambledon, with Agar on board, triggered an acoustic mine. The convoy promptly scattered, and was unable to regroup in the limited time available. Again Operation Lucid was reluctantly aborted. As if to add insult to injury, the return leg saw one oiler break down, and the other develop further faults.

Agar and Drax were keen to continue, and provisional plans were made to sail four seaworthy tankers on the night of November 1st/2nd. Alas it was not to be. On October 12th Hitler had postponed Sealion until the following spring, a decision immediately confirmed to British intelligence by virtue of ULTRA decrypts from Bletchley Park. The reduced threat of invasion meant that the considerable resources needed for each fireship sailing could no longer be justified, and in the face of worsening weather, Lucid was called off indefinitely.

Churchill remained enthusiastic, urging fireship 'Action This Day' in memos as late February 1941. Indeed records indicate that a Lucid II was planned that same month, a minute from Agar dated February 17th informing the Prime Minister that two fireships were at seven days' notice for offensive operations. Whether the operation sailed, and against what target, remains unclear. Curiously, Agar states in Footprints in the Sea that by the end of 1940 he had already left the fireship project for good, having lost his place in the queue of captains waiting for regular sea-commands and being 'again available for odd jobs that came along.' Quite why he omitted to mention that one such odd job was Lucid II remains a minor mystery.

Arguably, faint echoes of Lucid can been detected in the execution of the Saint-Nazaire raid in March 1942. Nineteen years later, Agar summed up the ill-starred fireship adventure thus:

> Looking back on Lucid I suppose we should be glad that it never came off, which is a mild way of saying it failed. First, because we might - and probably would - have lost half the crews of the fireships; and secondly because many German soldiers were spared the dreadful fate of perishing in flames. I can say quite definitely that the First Sea Lord was not over-enthusiastic about the operation, and this also applied to other senior officers in the Admiralty - but not all.

> I think the undercurrent of thought amongst the Naval Staff rated the operation as a side-show and were glad to be rid of it at the first opportunity. I know there were several sighs of relief when it was finally cancelled and the plan put into cold storage, lest it should be used against us. Imagine thousands of tons of burning oil floating up the Thames on a strong flood tide in the middle of heavy air raids on London! Such a feat was not impossible if resolute men volunteered to carry it out.

> On the other hand, the morale effect of a bold offensive stroke like Lucid would have helped a great deal to convince the United States and other neutrals that Britain was no 'quitter', and was determined at all costs to see the war out to the bitter end. From this we would have gained immeasurable prestige.

Alas, fate conspired to submerge immeasurable prestige in heroic failure. Lucid was quickly lost to history, and played no part in the subsequent development of the myth of a thwarted invasion attempt and burned German corpses.

In any event, that purpose had already been fulfilled by a far worse naval disaster 40 miles west of the Texel, in the North Sea.

THE TEXEL DISASTER

In September 1940 Mrs Pat Barnes was a schoolgirl living on a poultry farm in Crostwick Lane, Spixworth, near Norwich. In a letter to Anglia Television News in 1992 she recalled:

> For two days a convoy of army ambulances occupied this lane travelling slowly from North Walsham Road to Buxton Road, the drivers very grim-faced. We used to get a lot of army traffic through the lane, but nothing like this. Occasionally an army lorry would stop for eggs and also apples, and so the next time my mother asked what was going on two weeks before. She was told they had contained dead bodies of Germans washed up on the beach, as an invasion had been attempted. But that was all we were told. This picture has remained vivid in my memory. It seemed as though there were hundreds of trucks, going from nowhere to nowhere at walking pace.

The mysterious convoy is confirmed by John Baker White, in 1940 a major attached to the Directorate of Military Intelligence. In his aptly-titled memoir The Big Lie, published in 1955, he records several rumours of failed invasion, including:

> A convoy of ambulances arriving in the dead of night at a hospital outside Norwich, and an SOS sent to other hospitals in the area for anti-burn dressings. These were but a few of the forms the rumour took, and there are plenty of people in Britain who to this day remain convinced that there was an invasion attempt in 1940 and that it was defeated by setting the sea on fire.

The Norfolk story is a key piece in the jigsaw of the myth of a failed invasion attempt, for it can be stated with absolute confidence the vehicles seen moving westward along obscure roads north of the city in September 1940 were loaded with the survivors of a catastrophic North Sea disaster. Moreover the incident had left several hundred dead, and was hushed-up by the British authorities. However the casualties being driven towards Norwich were not survivors of a German invasion spearhead, but instead Royal Navy personnel from the 20th Destroyer Flotilla, a minelaying unit based at Immingham. Something of the truth is revealed by Stephen Roskill in The War at Sea. On the night of August 31st 1940, while the 20th Flotilla were laying mines in enemy-controlled waters, air reconnaissance reported an enemy force off the Dutch coast, steering west towards Britain. Fearing the onset of Sealion, the 20th Flotilla was ordered to intercept. In fact the enemy force comprised of nothing more dangerous than a small minelaying unit on passage from Cuxhaven to Rotterdam, but while on course to engage it the British destroyers ran into an uncharted minefield 40 miles north-west of the Texel. The Esk and Ivanhoe were sunk, the Express seriously damaged, and the Flotilla commander, Lieutenant-Commander Crouch, fatally injured.

That the loss of three valuable destroyers was the result of an abortive anti-invasion dash was confirmed by Sir John Colville, then private secretary to Churchill. In his journal, published as The Fringes of Power, Colville noted on August 31st that:

> After dinner the First Lord rang up to say that enemy ships were steering westwards from Terschelling. The invasion may be pending (though I'll lay 10-1 against!) and all HM Forces are taking up their positions. If these German ships come on they would reach the coast of Norfolk tomorrow morning.

Neither account gives any real idea of the true cost of the Texel disaster. The Esk sank immediately with the loss of Crouch and all but one of her 150-strong crew, while Express had her bows blown off, with the result that Captain JG Bickford and 90 other personnel were killed or fatally wounded. While taking off wounded from Express, Ivanhoe was mined herself, leaving 53 dead and the bulk of her crew injured. After attempts to scuttle Ivanhoe failed she was torpedoed by an MTB on September 1st. Several life-rafts from the ships drifted into the Dutch coast, where their occupants were taken prisoner. Altogether the combined death toll amounted to almost 300, and the total casualty figure (including wounded and prisoners) closer to 400. Only during the Dunkirk evacuation had the Nore Command suffered worse casualties in a single day. The casualty lists, released to the press on September 13th, make for harrowing reading.

The fate of the survivors of this ill-starred engagement was revealed by Don Tate, in 1940 a young naval rating based at Great Yarmouth. On the evening of September 2nd Tate visited a local cinema, and on his return to barracks at 10.30pm:

> I was asked to assist with Royal Navy survivors who were soon to be landed. Others were being rounded up around the town in similar fashion. I went immediately to the harbour and waited with the others, excitedly wondering what it was all about.

After an hour or more, the first ship came alongside with survivors - all of them RN personnel. The last ship in I recall was in the early hours of the 3rd. We dealt with the survivors how and wherever we could help - carrying a few wounded ashore, supplying blankets to those without clothing, passing around food and cigarettes, as well as listing names and numbers.

All the while we helped we talked to them, and I naturally asked many what had happened at sea that night. Repeatedly the answer came that they had been 'attacking barges' when, in the confusion, the ship struck a mine. A second ship, moving in to help the first, had also become mined. A few of the survivors that night also said that the RAF had been dropping oil bombs. Those who said that were in the minority, but all were emphatic that they had attacked barges.

When time permitted I asked some of the more talkative where this incident had taken place, but there was a considerable amount of confusion on this point. I later learned from actions at sea in which I was personally involved that this uncertainty can be quite commonplace, since a crew is not given a running commentary. If the pace is hectic and the action period fairly drawn out, then position becomes almost lost as far as the crew is concerned.

What happened next is not difficult to reconstruct, and chimes exactly with the ambulance convoy mentioned by Baker White, and observed first-hand by the Barnes family in Spixworth. The Texel survivors were landed not by one vessel but by several, and over an extended period. Whether the local hospital facilities in Yarmouth were inadequate, or because it was felt that their presence in the immediate area would be bad both for service and civilian morale, many casualties from the 20th Flotilla were transferred to hospitals inland. This transfer lasted several days. Again for reasons of morale, and of understandable secrecy, obscure roads such as Crostwick Lane were favoured. Such an unusual event naturally attracted attention, but instead of revealing to civilians that a substantial number of their own side had become casualties of a false alarm, what better placebo than disinformation that the convoy carried what remained of a thwarted German invasion force?

The Admiralty admitted something of the Texel disaster as early as September 6th, revealing that survivors had been landed 'at an East Coast port' and transferred to hospitals. Within days the incident had became confused in the public mind with the celebrated 'Cromwell' invasion alarm on Saturday September 7th, an air raid warden in Ipswich recording a exaggerated rumour in circulation by Sunday that the Esk and Ivanhoe had been 'part of a task force of 160 ships sent to Holland where concentrations of troops were reported.' A week later, the Barnes family were pitched a still more heartening spin on the story, which transformed disaster into victory, and which proves conclusively that the myth of a failed invasion attempt was deliberately contrived and distributed, as we shall see in the following two chapters.

The Texel Disaster: the destroyer Express, with her bows blown off by a mine, seen from the forecastle of Kelvin on September 1st 1940. The loss of two destroyers, and the landing of survivors at east coast ports, fuelled rumours of a German landing attempt in early September. (IWM)

'BEACHES BLACK WITH BODIES'
1940: The Invasion that Failed

At 8.07 pm on the evening of Saturday September 7th 1940, GHQ Home Forces in London flashed the codeword 'Cromwell' to Eastern and Southern Commands, to indicate that invasion was probable within the next 12 hours. It is said that a number of factors combined to trigger this major alert, including tidal conditions, the onset of the first mass air raid on London, and the landing of several ill-prepared German spies on the Kent coast four days before. The result was widespread panic and alarm across the entire country, with church bells rung and bridges blown, in the mistaken belief that the invasion was actually underway.

Vague speculation over enemy landings in Britain had already appeared in the Daily Herald at the end of August, and the Daily Mirror on September 3rd. However, the 'Cromwell' scare, together with the visible aftermath of the Texel disaster in Norfolk a week earlier, resulted in British newspapers reporting further rumours of an invasion attempt, despite the best efforts of the censor. On September 12th the Glasgow Herald ran a story culled from the previous day's New York Sun, which hinted at a 'suicidal' thrust at the west of England launched from St Malo. On the 14th the Daily Mirror carried another secondhand story from an American newsagency source:

INVASION TROOPS DIE IN SEA: The Germans have already tried to invade England at different points and failed, an American surgeon who has arrived in New York from Lisbon stated yesterday. Doctor Charles Bove, head surgeon of the American Hospital in Paris, said he saw hundreds of German bodies in the water near Cherbourg - presumably the bodies of men taking part in an attempted invasion of England.

'All along the French coast the Germans are constantly practising for invasion,' he added. 'They set out on ships and are made to leap overboard and swim considerable distances with all their equipment.'

The effect of these reports on anxious British civilians is clear from the diary of Ipswich air raid warden Richard Brown. On September 13th Brown recorded of the Cromwell alert:

What is the secret of last Saturday's affair? New York now has rumours that

Jerry corpses were being washed up on the Yarmouth beaches in quantities. Green says 30,000 of them, but I should have thought they'd be too weighty with equipment to do anything but sink.

Two days later, on the 15th, Brown continued:

Re that last entry, I'm beginning to think a real attempt was made, not a rehearsal. The American report concerns an attack from St Malo on the west coast of England. Harry says another was made on Scotland, and it's pretty definite that bodies were washed up on these beaches.

Coverage of the St Malo report, and Dr Bove's unlikely story, prompted a formal denial from the War Office on September 15th. The following day the Daily Telegraph reported:

AXIS WEAKENS ON INVASION - RUMOUR DENIED: It was stated by the War Office yesterday that there was no foundation for the stories in circulation to the effect that an actual attempt at invading this country had been made by the Germans. These stories have been of a circumstantial kind. In one the enemy was supposed to have landed a force which was immediately overcome. Another made the suggestion that large numbers of dead invaders had been picked up off the Goodwins.

In America, unfettered by censorship, the fourth estate ignored the War Office denial. On September 17th, beneath the headline REPULSE IS REPORTED, the New York Times published a report based on an Associated Press wire from Lisbon, the capitol of neutral Portugal and already a key centre of intelligence and espionage activity. The article ran thus:

Lisbon, Portugal, September 16 (AP) - British informants arriving here by plane from London declared today that a small-scale German attempt at a landing somewhere along the English coast last week was beaten off with heavy losses to the would-be invaders. They were unable to give the exact time and place, but asserted that they were convinced of the accuracy of their information. 'British coastal artillery and small patrol craft played havoc with German barges,' one of the British informants said here, 'and not a single German reached land alive. Scores of bodies are reported still being washed up on our shores.' The informant agreed the landing attempt - if it had been made - was not a full-dress attempt at invasion but perhaps designed to test British defences.

It is a matter of historical record that Operation Sealion did not weigh anchor in September 1940, or at any other time. Why then in London did the War Office deny reports of a landing, when in Lisbon and New York quasi-official sources were keen to talk up the very same rumour? And if no landing attempt had been made, why were a considerable number of dead German soldiers washed up on the south coast of England shortly afterwards? For despite subsequent attempts to discredit the story, there exists hard evidence that several dozen Wehrmacht corpses were in fact recovered.

Towards the end of September, William Robinson, a Royal Artillery gunner stationed at Herne Bay with 333 Coastal Artillery Battery, was sent to Folkestone to take part in a macabre detail. Together with half a dozen others, he was instructed to search the beach between Hythe and St Mary's Bay for dead Germans. On the first day two such bodies were located, together with seven or eight more over the next two days. All were taken by truck to a field west of New Romney, where they were unloaded behind a canvas screen. An NCO checked the corpses for identity discs and paybooks, which were in turn handed over to an officer. Robinson recognised the dead men as German soldiers, rather than airmen or naval personnel, by their field-grey uniforms. All appeared to have been in the water for some time. By way of reward for discharging this unpleasant duty Robinson and his colleagues drew a daily ration of 20 Woodbines, and additional daily pay of two shillings.

Robinson recounted his story on a BBC television programme, Their Finest Hour, in November 1957. Repeating his account to the Daily Mail, he added that the uniforms worn by the dead men bore no insignia, and that he believed they had died during an exercise. There is no reason to believe that Robinson was lying, for bodies continued to arrive on the Dungeness peninsula for at least another month. On October 22nd the Times and other papers reported that:

The body of a German soldier was washed ashore yesterday at Littlestone on the Kent coast. He was wearing the uniform of a German infantry regiment and appeared to be about 28. The body had been in the sea for several weeks and death is believed to have been due to drowning.

The war diary of the 5th Battalion Somerset Light Infantry confirms that the body was actually found on the 20th. Over the same weekend the remains of a Luftwaffe airman were recovered slightly further to the west. The retrieval of the soldier's remains at Littlestone was also announced on the BBC evening news, while on October 26th the Folkestone, Hythe and District Herald added:

An examination of the body left no doubt as to its identity. The man, aged about 30, was wearing the field- grey uniform of a German infantry unit, and he was probably an NCO. The body, it was estimated, had been in the sea possibly as long as six weeks, and such a period fits in with the report recently published that the RAF inflicted severe losses on the German invasion troops on the other side of the Channel at about that time. There were no signs of injury externally. Arrangements were made to bury the dead man at New Romney.

Today the grave of Heinrich Poncke, of Anti-Tank Reserve Company 19, can be visited at the Deutsche Soldatenfriedhof at Cannock Chase, Staffordshire. Poncke did not perish while attempting to invade Britain, nor was he one of thousands of similar casualties. He instead drowned either while training for Operation Sealion, or (as seems likely) during a successful Royal Navy 'cutting-out' operation against German flak trawlers moored in the Channel on October 11th. Three Felixstowe-based motor torpedo boats, using Dover as a forward base, sank two such trawlers north of Calais and captured a total of 34 crewmen, several others being drowned. Over the next few weeks Poncke's body was carried by the tide to Littlestone, with others arriving elsewhere, and on both sides of the Channel. This tends to confirm the truth of an official statement made in the House of Commons in 1946, in which Clement Attlee stated that the bodies of 'about 36' German soldiers had been washed up at scattered points on the coast between Cornwall and Great Yarmouth over a period of four to six weeks in September and October 1940.

Wildfire rumours of the 'invasion that failed' owed much to the chance conjunction of factual events such as the Texel disaster, the Cromwell alarm, and the arrival of scattered corpses, including aircrew. However, it owed rather more to deliberate fabrication by an ad hoc (and hitherto unacknowledged) amalgamation of astute British propagandists, political warfare experts and intelligence personnel, variously attached to MI6, the Petroleum Warfare Department, the Directorate of Military Intelligence and the Special Operations Executive. Indeed so potent was the rumour, and so secret the means of dissemination, that years later it would return to excite national media controversy in 1957 and 1992.

The only public document which gives any real detail of the creation and dissemination of the myth is The Big Lie, a memoir by John Baker White published in 1955. Baker White, a somewhat eccentric individual, had formed his own cell to fight communist and occult influence in British society during the 1930s, and is not an entirely reliable witness. Moreover his book was published at a time when all such texts were tightly constrained by official

Re-creation of the recovery of one of the 'bodies on the beach' during the summer/autumn of 1940.

41

secrecy, and while Baker White was the serving Conservative MP for Canterbury. It does, however, carry some authority. In 1940 Baker White was a major serving with the Directorate of Military Intelligence under the newly appointed DMI, Major-General FJ 'Paddy' Beaumont-Nesbitt. Nesbitt was convinced that Germany would attempt an invasion of the British Isles, even going to far to inform the Joint Intelligence Committee in September that 'anyone who says the Germans will not invade is mad.' In August, Baker White was assigned to a small DMI sub-section operating from offices in Berkeley Square, whose brief was the delivery of propaganda and disinformation to enemy troops. Although Baker White does not say so, his post clearly also included liaison with similar departments in secret service organisations such as MI5, MI6 and SOE, as well as the Ministry of Information and the BBC:

> Our task was not to stop the Germans finding out about the real state of our defences. That was the job of the security agencies. What we had to do was to create in the minds of the German High Command and of Hitler himself a completely fictitious picture of what they would have to face if they launched an invasion attempt. A picture of a powerfully armed Britain, and above all armed with new weapons of terrible destructive power. We had to put over the Big Lie.

> We know today that the aim was achieved. A combination formed of the vigilance of the RAF and our security forces blindfolded the German Staff planners and compelled Hitler to seek information from rumours culled from the secret reports of hundreds of Gestapo and Abwehr agents in neutral countries. By methods that must remain for ever secret, Britain supplied many of the rumours.

> I cannot say today, any more than I could have said at the time, how the thought and the wish became a rumour that was to go around the world. Certainly I do not claim complete authorship. I believe that, as in the case of so many successful rumours, it was not any one man's invention but was born from conversation between two or three people devoting their thoughts and discussion to the same question.

> Before the rumour was fed into the pipeline that ran to the bar of the Grand Hotel in Stockholm, the Avenida in Lisbon, the Ritz in Madrid, and other places in Cairo, Istanbul, Ankara and elsewhere, not forgetting New York, it had to get over certain hurdles, including the committee that had to study all rumours before they were launched. This was a very necessary precaution,

because it was quite possible for the rumour inventors to manufacture a story that would quite unwittingly disclose something of operational importance.

In 1955 strict official secrecy prevented Baker White from revealing any further detail of the 'two or three people', the 'rumour inventors', the 'committee' or the 'pipeline' which ensured the success of the myth of the failed invasion. Working backwards, however, the passage of the rumour in all its variants can be traced through the primitive intelligence networks extant in 1940 like a barium meal.

During the First World War, Britain had come to recognise the value of organised propaganda relatively late. Legends of 1914 such as the phantom bowmen at Mons, and the 'Russians in England' with snow on their boots, were the result of happy accident, while later variants of the Mons legend involving angels and Christ-like battlefield helpers were simply romantic fantasy. After 1918 the black art of political warfare was variously ignored by the War Office, or left to the Secret Intelligence Service, MI6. Only in 1938 did the Committee of Imperial Defence, then chaired by the omnipresent Lord Hankey, draft plans for an independent Propaganda to the Enemy Department. Its first director was Sir Campbell Stuart, a Great War veteran subsequently employed as managing editor of both the Times and the Daily Mail. Funded by MI6, the new section was allocated premises at Electra House on Victoria Embankment, and thus christened Department EH.

In 1938 the Munich Crisis prompted the printing of a large number of leaflets. Although none were dropped over Germany, this dry-run was not without value, for on October 4th EH despatched a note to the Air Ministry, the recipient of which was Sir Donald Banks, then a Permanent Secretary, and later Director-General of the Petroleum Warfare Department. According to EH, the 'sharpest and most urgent lesson' taught by the Munich 'dress rehearsal' was the need for 'properly co-ordinated arrangements for the conveyance of information into enemy countries.' As events the following year clearly demonstrate, Banks evidently took note.

On September 1st 1939, two days before war was declared, Department EH was mobilized to Woburn Abbey, and joined there initially by a propaganda team from Section D, an MI6 sub-section charged with 'unavowable' subversion activity of foreign territories. Although in September 1939 close on 20 million leaflets were delivered by aircraft, during the Phoney War EH had a negligible effect on the developing conflict. Much of the work was as moribund as the war itself until May 1940, the Department being almost exclusively concerned with the creation of overt 'white' rather than covert 'black' propaganda. One unlikely suggestion fielded in March was a scheme to project huge magic lantern images over the German lines. Another turned upon the widespread (but false) belief that Hitler believed in astrology. The proposal that a well-known astrologer should provide 'a horoscope of Hitler predicting disaster for him and his country and putting it into Germany by secret channels' was later implemented, notably by way of an American lecture tour in 1941 by the exiled Hungarian charlatan Louis de Wohl.

June 1940 saw the evacuation of the BEF from Dunkirk, the capitulation of France, and the ousting of Campbell Stuart as head of EH. His successor, Hugh Dalton, was a senior Labour politician who Churchill had appointed Minister of Economic Warfare after forming his coalition government in May. Two months later, on July 16th, Churchill invited Dalton to take charge of a new organisation, the Special Operations Executive (SOE), whose task was to coordinate acts of subversion and sabotage in enemy-occupied territory. Famously, Churchill ordered SOE to 'set Europe ablaze', and against this background it seems fitting that the original SOE summit meeting on July 1st was attended by Lord Hankey, Geoffrey Lloyd and Desmond Morton - three men instrumental in the founding of the Petroleum Warfare Department just eight days later. Also present at the SOE summit was the DMI, Paddy Beaumont-Nesbitt, to whom Baker White reported.

Here, then, are revealed at least some of the 'rumour inventors' identified by Baker White in addition to his own four- man section. SOE formally came into being on July 22nd and was at first an amalgamation, comprising Department EH, Section D, and MI(R), a small sub-branch of the Directorate of Military Intelligence concerned with irregular warfare. Dalton's new hybrid was divided in two: SO(2) were charged with Deeds, chiefly subversion and sabotage in the field; while SO(1) would deal with Words, or propaganda. Since no SOE networks yet existed abroad, at this time the 'pipeline' by which unavowable black rumours were spread chiefly comprised MI6 outstations operating under cover of British legations in neutral capitols such as Stockholm, Geneva, Ankara, Madrid and Lisbon, as well as the social venues listed by Baker White.

The other key link in the pipeline was New York, from where Allied propaganda could be spread across America via radio, newspapers and key syndicated columnists. This vital function was fulfilled by British Security Co-ordination, the New York MI6 station codenamed Intrepid and run by Sir William Stephenson from June 1940 onwards. BSC was charged with three principal tasks, these being the procurement of war materials, political lobbying, and to counteract German propaganda activity in the United States. The official history of BSC, written in 1945 and classified until 1998, makes no mention of any BSC involvement in promulgating the failed invasion myth in

1940. However, Intrepid also housed SOE and MI6 representatives, and the text does make explicit that BSC was able to 'initiate internal propaganda through its undercover contacts with selected newspapers', including the New York Times, New York Herald Tribune and Baltimore Sun. The official BSC history also acknowledged several named individuals who rendered 'service of particular value', including New York Times president AH Sulzberger and journalist/commentator William Shirer. The particular significance of Shirer, the respected author of Berlin Diary and The Rise and fall of the Third Reich, will become clear in the following chapter.

In the Big Lie, Baker White concentrates almost exclusively on the burning sea rumour, which did not surface in its common form until November 1940. Less extravagant rumours of a thwarted landing and bodies on beaches first surfaced in strength in the wake of the then-inexplicable 'Cromwell' invasion alert on September 7th, but at this stage none spoke of charred bodies or burning oil. One such rumour told of a landing in Sandwich Bay, where the inshore waters were said to be 'black' with German dead, later buried secretly in the sand dunes. A diarist in the Suffolk town of Bury St Edmunds recorded the corpse rumour as early as September 12th, another in Ipswich the following day. According to the regional diary kept by the Home Guard in Cornwall, the 15th was the first occasion on which 'we heard reports of bodies washed ashore all along the south coast.' British reports based on reports from New York papers prompted a robust denial from the War Office on the 15th, and the Daily Telegraph to the record the rumours of large numbers of German dead on the Goodwin Sands. Already the story had taken on a life of its own, and despite Regulation 39b on September 30th the Daily Herald even gave space to a scare story that the Isle of Wight had been overrun.

The military too took note, an 11 Corps summary of 'rumours and indiscreet talk' dated September 25th revealing:

15 Division report the currency in their area of a rumour that the bodies of thousands of German soldiers have been washed up on the beach at Clacton. The source of this can not at present be traced.

In the same North Essex sector, a 45th Infantry Brigade Intelligence Summary reported:

It has been noticed, particularly during the last month, that rumours of a spectacular nature have been very widespread. The following were the principal ones noticed:

(i) nearly all troops in the Sub-Area have heard the rumour that thousands of bodies of German troops were washed up on the South Coast of England in the early part of the month.

(ii) Another rumour, not so widespread, is that an invasion by sea was started but was destroyed before reaching this country.

The origins of these rumours are difficult to trace but the majority of them are thought to have originated from civilian sources, ie correspondence from friends and relations.

At Southend-on-Sea, it was whispered, the enemy remains had been collected in corporation dustcarts. One man allegedly told a reporter:

The fact is that the whole coastline is in the occupation of the military authorities. If they thought it was necessary to conceal the dead bodies of Germans they would have no difficulty. For myself, it is enough that closed lorries going to and from the beach at one point and mysterious ambulances at another, are indications that out- of-the-ordinary things have been happening.

With the benefit of hindsight, this roving eyewitness bears the hallmarks of a press invention, conjured to vent Fleet Street spleen at the official embargo on reporting the invasion rumours. Indeed it does seem perverse that the British press were firmly discouraged from reporting such a heartening story. In Blue Pencil Admiral, a memoir published in 1947 by the chief press censor, Rear-Admiral George Thomson, the following rationale is offered:

From the censorship point of view, the undesirability of reports that an invasion had actually been attempted is obvious. For, resolute though the people of Britain were, there is no getting away from the fact that we were preparing to defend Britain with 50 tanks and 200 field guns, some of them taken from museums. And in these ticklish circumstances anything which might create 'alarm and despondency' was to be avoided.

In truth Thomson's reasoning is hardly obvious at all, bearing in mind that he states elsewhere that there was 'no security objection' to the failed invasion story being printed. Probably the denials were prompted more by political expediency, and the need to maintain the belief in America that Britain was still under threat of invasion, and thus still in need of urgent military supplies. Whatever the reason, Thomson added:

The truth or falsity of statements submitted is not the legitimate concern of the censor. His business is to prevent the enemy obtaining valuable information. In the case of the 'invasion that failed'... each time I received a story about it I rang up the editor of the paper concerned and assured him most emphatically that it was not true. In every case where this happened the editor took my word and did not publish the story. But nothing I could do prevented it from cropping up again and again. And under our voluntary system of censorship it was impossible to prevent publication in every case, for there was obviously no security objection, and some of the stories were not submitted.

The successive landing and body rumours spread around the world with astonishing speed, thanks largely to advanced American wire service technology. In this way, a rumour devised at Woburn or Whitehall and launched in Zurich could find its way back to London via New York or Chicago, to be published in slightly different form in the Mirror or the Telegraph. According to Ellic Howe, in his masterly study The Black Game, by late September 1940 the output of rumours by British agencies had begun to exceed the capacity of the pipeline to disseminate them. The following selection from the BSC-friendly New York Times, doubtless devised with no little merriment, reflect those passed for flotation abroad. They include those black elements most frequently encountered in reports from neutral territories, which were repeated by some British editors in defiance of the censor:

NAZI DEAD SAID TO HALT FISHING : London, September 28th (UP) - A Scottish family received a letter today from a relative in Sweden reporting that Swedish fisherman were forced to abandon herring fisheries because the bodies of many German soldiers were floating in the waters off the southern coast of Sweden. The letter said the German authorities had offered a reward of about 75 cents for each body recovered with the uniform intact.

NAZI LOSSES SEEN IN INVASION DRILLS - The Germans have suffered severe losses in exercises and manoeuvres in the English Channel preparatory to an invasion attempt, according to passengers who arrived [from Lisbon] on the Exeter of the American Export Line. One estimate was that 10,000 men had been lost. 'The German soldiers,' said one passenger, who refused to give his name because he has relatives living in Holland, 'were heavily armed and weighted down with full equipment. They were taken a mile or so to sea off the Netherlands coast aboard flat-bottomed boats. The boats would come toward shore and the men were forced to leap out and swim. We people living near the sea saw thousands of floating bodies of officers and men floating in the water. Many soldiers rebelled and were chained and taken back to the interior of Germany to be punished for their insubordination.'

LETTER TO THE EDITOR FROM NORWAY: In Oslo truckloads of German soldiers - tied and bound - pass in the streets on their way to Fort Akershus, where they would rather be shot than drowned. The reason being that they refuse to invade England in the little boats much too small to cross the North Sea ...They have received a severe handling by the RAF. German losses in Cherbourg are estimated at between 40,000 and 50,000 killed and wounded. Almost every civil and military hospital from the Belgian to the Spanish frontier has been requisitioned. I understand that more than 12,000 wounded German soldiers occupy Bordeaux hospitals and approximately 7000 are in Paris. The majority of the one-time fashionable hotels at Biarritz are now either convalescent homes or hospitals.

By October, identical reports of packed hospitals and manacled mutineers extended the length of the invasion coast, from Oslo to Antwerp to Le Havre. As common were tales of heavy air raids, catastrophe at sea and miserly cash rewards for the retrieval of bodies and uniforms. In death, as in life, it was hinted, the Nazi regime attached little value to humanity. In truth, all were shrewd fabrications by British propagandists channelled through the extemporised pipeline, and frequently opportunistic in nature. Just as the aftermath of the Texel disaster was passed off in Norfolk as a secret victory, so too were other coincidental events, such as the flak trawler raid on October 11th which probably killed Heinrich Poncke. Of this operation Baker White further records:

The other stroke of luck was even greater... Shortly after dawn, the Royal Navy put ashore at Dover the trawler crew and ten rather bewildered German soldiers. As soon as he looked at their pay books and interrogated them, the Intelligence officer realised that the ten men were drawn from eight different units. Someone jumped to the significance of this fact from the point of view of political warfare and a supporting deception for the burning sea rumour. The same evening, in the German Forces Programme, and in the ordinary German civilian programme from London it was announced that ten soldiers had been brought into Dover that morning unhurt, 'rescued from the sea.' Their full names, numbers and unit identifications were given. The announcement closed with the words: 'We know nothing of the fate of their comrades,' followed by funeral music from Wagner.

This obscure incident no doubt contributed greatly to the mid-September mystery, but passed unreported at the time. Instead the Big Lie was lent more widespread credibility by the arrival in New York from Lisbon of carefully primed passengers on board liners. Among the more interesting reports was that run by the New York Times on September 21st:

Robert Solberg, returning with his wife and daughter after 20 years of residence in France, said the Germans were holding invasion practice off the French coast also. He asserted, as did other passengers, that the Dutch and the French were supplying the British with advance information of German exercises on self-propelled barges in the Channel and that British bombers had taken a heavy toll.

Mr Solberg added that he had definite information that the Germans have attempted no actual invasion of England. He said the British, tipped off by the Dutch and French, waited for the barges with planes and submarines and that 'thousands of Germans have been lost in this fashion.' Mr Solberg said he recently visited a French Channel port where bodies of German troops were being washed ashore daily.

On the same date a Daily Mail correspondent in New York teased further details from Mr Solberg, here described as the vice-president of a steel company. Having left France on August 25th, he stated:

The British sent submarines and planes and sank the barges. It is estimated that at least 10,000 Germans lost their lives. Many of the German troops are refusing to continue the practice and hundreds are being transported back to Germany with their hands tied behind their backs. When these prison trains cross the border into Germany, air raid alarms are sounded to drive people underground so that they will not see Nazi soldiers in disgrace.

These reports are particularly telling, for Robert Solberg (the correct spelling) was no ordinary refugee, and was reading from a script penned by British intelligence. Solborg, a former Czarist cavalry officer, had fled the Bolshevik revolution in 1917. Having acquired American citizenship before the outbreak of the Second World War, Solborg joined American military intelligence in December 1940, and in October 1941 was sent to London in his capacity as chief of the special operations section of CO1 (later OSS), the US military intelligence agency headed by Colonel William Donovan. Solborg's three-month assignment in 1941 was to study the methods employed by SOE, and advise Donovan accordingly. Donovan had made his own visit to Britain in July 1940, and by September was already well aware of the PWD's experimental flame warfare programme. Solborg, in turn, was well placed to complete his report on SOE the following year, since in Lisbon they (or SIS) had primed him with the 'corpse' misinformation imparted on his arrival in New York on board the Exeter. The American surgeon Charles Bove was evidently briefed in similar fashion.

Solborg's story is easy to dissect at 60 years' remove. He had not been resident in France for 20 years, and at this early stage in the war Dutch and French patriots were not involved in sophisticated resistance work of the kind described. That fabrication is probably instead a cover for ULTRA signal decoding activity at Bletchley Park. In fact RAF bombing of the invasion ports was surprisingly ineffectual, and certainly did not result in the loss of 'thousands' of German troops, either on land or at sea. Furthermore, Solborg would not have been allowed near the occupied coastline during this period unless as part of a supervised press party, a process described by William Shirer in his Berlin Diary. Even if Solborg had visited such a port, he would scarcely have been permitted to observe bodies washed ashore. The stories of manacled mutineers are lifted straight from the then-current military intelligence myth catalogue. Finally, the firm denial that any actual landing had been attempted in England is consistent with the official line from the War Office, and confirmed by the censor, Rear-Admiral Thomson.

Nonetheless, by the end of September 1940 most newspapers in neutral countries, and in particular the United States, were running stories of a failed landing with marked alacrity. The substance of the reports was that Germany had lost 30,000 to 60,000 troops in a disaster on about September 16th, when RAF bombing and a Channel gale conspired to scatter the Sealion fleet. The contribution made by Bomber Command seemed to be confirmed by an Air Ministry News Service bulletin issued on the evening of October 18th, which was widely quoted at home and abroad. Mass mutinies added extra zest, while the innate absurdity of the idea that Hitler had lost half his invasion force was obscured by the fog of war and credulity. So persistent were the rumours in Europe and America that Berlin was finally obliged to issue the first of several formal denials.

CHANNEL LOSSES DENIED: Berlin, September 25th (AP) - Authorised German sources said today that there was no truth in reports that many thousands of bodies of German soldiers were being washed ashore along the English Channel. Such accounts were declared to be an indication of a situation that compels the British 'to put out such silly lies.'

It is recorded elsewhere that the Sicherheitsdienst, the SS security service, expressed surprise that exaggerated casualty figures of 60,000 were not in themselves sufficient to convince the civilian population in Germany that the story was self-evidently absurd. Following the Air Ministry bulletin the following month, and a further rash of lurid reports typified by a lengthy New York Sun piece on October 7th which described 'hundreds of flat-bottomed barges... raked by withering fire... leaving the Channel filled with bodies and wreckage', Berlin issued another firm denial:

> Berlin, October 18th (AP): Authorised German sources said today that 'nothing is known' here about any foiling of a German invasion attempt to invade Great Britain by British air attacks on transports in the Channel harbours, as reported by British authorities.

Although the burning sea variant had not yet been reported in the press, an early prototype would seem to have been launched into the pipeline as early as September 15th. William Shirer, then with Columbia Broadcasting, was visiting Geneva on September 16th. In his Berlin Diary, published in book form the following year, Shirer noted that:

> The news coming over the border of France is that the Germans have attempted a landing in Britain, but that it has been repulsed with heavy German losses. Must take these with a pinch of salt... The stories there were that either in attempted German raids with sizeable landing parties on the English coast or in rehearsals with boats and barges off the French coast the British had given the Germans a bad pummelling. The reports reaching Switzerland from France were that many German barges and ships had been destroyed and a considerable number of German troops drowned; also that the British used a new type of wireless- directed torpedo which spread ignited oil on the water and burned the barges.

Similarly, at about the same time British prisoners-of-war held captive in Germany heard via the 'latrinogram':

> A fine crop [of rumour] about the supposed invasion of England; that 80,000 Germans had attempted to land and had been drowned in the Wash; that a strong naval attacking force had been completely routed by the skill of our own submarines which had spread oil on the sea around it and had then set fire to the oil.

The latter scheme was technically feasible, as the anti-seaplane trials with L.26 in April 1940 had demonstrated, although rumours involving submarines and oil torpedoes are more likely to have been a fiction suggested by Lord Hankey. Indeed these bear a striking similarities with his 'Greek Fire' scheme put forward in 1915 for use at Gallipoli, as detailed in the Chapter One.

In September 1940 not a yard of coastal flame barrage had been installed by Petroleum Warfare Department, the existence of which was still a closely guarded secret. Its experimental trials were concluded in full view of the enemy, as demonstrated by the south coast trials at Dumpton on July 3rd, Dungeness on the 6th, and at Titchfield on August 24th. PWD involvement is also evident in two related examples of overt 'white' propaganda directed at German invasion troops in October 1940. The first was an aircraft leaflet dropped over enemy-occupied invasion ports. Titled Wir Fahren Gegen Engelland, the text appeared in French, Dutch and German, and was intended for consumption by friendly civilians also. A facsimile of this 'Short Invasion Phrasebook' is reproduced elsewhere in this book, but of particular interest is section two:

DURING THE INVASION:
1. The sea crossing - storm - fog - gale.
2. We feel seasick. Where is the bucket?
3. Is that a bomb - torpedo - grenade - mine?
4. Look out! English motor torpedo boats - destroyers - cruisers - battleships - bombers!
5. Our boat has capsized - sunk - BURNT - exploded!
6. Our squad - platoon - company - battalion - regiment is going under!
7. The others - the whole division - the entire army corps - too!
8. Another ship is beginning to sink.
9. Where is our fleet - our air force?
10. THE SEA SMELLS OF PETROL HERE!
11. THE SEA EVEN BURNS HERE!
12. SEE HOW WELL THE CAPTAIN BURNS!
13. Karl - Willi - Fritz - Johann - Abraham : CREMATED - drowned - minced by the propellors!
14. We must turn back!
15. Wir fahren gegen Engelland! (worse luck)

These same elements were adapted for radio broadcast by Sefton Delmer on the BBC's German service. In 1941 Delmer would take over responsibility for all black propaganda activity undertaken by the Political Warfare Executive, but in September 1940 was confined to broadcasting 'cheerful little talks full of

DER KLEINE
INVASIONS-
DOLMETSCHER

PETIT MANUEL
DE CONVERSATION
POUR L'INV ' SION

TAALCURSUS
ZONDER LEERMEESTEP
VOOR DUITSCHE SOLD '

I. Vor der Invasion

1. Die See ist gross — kalt — stürmisch.
2. Wie oft müssen wir noch Landungsmanöver üben?
3. Ob wir wohl in England ankommen werden ?
4. Ob wir heil zurückkommen werden ?

5. Wann ist der nächste englische Luftangriff? Heute morgens ; mittags ; nachmittags; abends; nachts.

6. Warum fährt der Führer nicht mit?

7. Unser Benzinlager brennt noch immer!

8. Euer Benzinlager brennt schon wieder !

9. War hat schon wieder das Telefonkabel durchgeschnitten !
10. Haben Sie meinen Kameraden in den Kanal geworfen!
11. Können Sie mir eine Schwimmweste — einen Rettungsring — leihen?
12. Was kosten bei Ihnen Schwimmstunden?

13. Wie viele Invasionsfahrten brauch' ich für das E.K.I ?

14. Sieben — acht — neun.
15. Wir werden gegen Engelland fahren !

I. Avant l'invasion

1. La mer est vaste — froide — houleuse.
2. Combien de fois encore devrons-nous faire des exercises de débarquement?
3. Pensez-vous que nous arriverons jamais en Angleterre?
4. Pensez-vous que nous reviendrons jamais d'Angleterre?
5. Quand le prochain raid anglais aura-t-il lieu? — Aujourd'hui, dans la matinée, à midi, dans l'après-midi, dans la soirée, dans la nuit.
6. Pourquoi est-ce que le Fuehrer ne vient pas avec nous?
7. Notre dépôt d'essence continue de brüler !
8. Votre dépôt d'essence a recommencé à brüler !
9. Qui a encore coupé notre ligne téléphonique?
10. Avez-vous jeté mon camarade dans le canal?
11. Pouvez-vous me prêter une ceinture, — une bouée de sauvetage?
12. Quel prix prenez-vous pour les leçons de natation?
13. Combien d'invasions dois-je faire pour recevoir la Croix de Fer de Ière classe?
14. Sept — huit — neuf.
15. Nous partirons pour l'Angleterre ! (Qu'ils disent.)

I. Vóór de invasie

1. De zee is groot — koud — stormachtig.
2. Hoe vaak nog moeten w'exerceeren om 't landen op een kust te leeren ?
3. Zullen we ooit in Engeland komen ?

4. Zullen we heelhuids wèerom komen ?

5. Wanneer komt de volgende Britsche luchtaanval ? Heden — morgen, middag, namiddag, avond, nacht.

6. Waarom reist de Führer niet met ons mee ?
7. Ons benzinedepot staat nog steeds in lichter laaie !
8. Uw benzinedepot staat alweer in lichter laaie !
9. Wie heeft nu telefoonleiding nou weer doo geknipt ?
10. Heeft J mijn eraan in de gracht gesme ?
11. Kan U mij een zwemvest — een reddinggordel leenen ?
12. Hoeveel kost het om bij U zwemmen te leeren ?
13. Hoe dikwijls moet ik aan een invasietocht meedoen om het IJzeren Kruis te winnen ?
14. Zeven — acht — negen keer.
15. Wij zullen gauw naar Engeland varen ! (Plons ! Plons ! Plons !)

II. Wahrend der Invasion

1. Der Seegang. — Der Sturm. — Der Nebel. Die Windstärke.
2. Wir sind seekrank. Wo ist der Kübel!

3. Ist das eine Bombe — ein Torpedo — eine Granate — eine Mine ?

II. Pendant l'invasion

1. Le gros temps — la tempête — le brouillard — la violence de l'ouragan.
2. Nous avons le mal de mer. Où est la cuvette?
3. Est-ce une bombe — une torpille — un obus — une mine?

II. Tijdens de invasie

1. De deining — de storm — de mist — de orkaan.
2. Wij zijn zeeziek. Waar is de kwispedoor ?
3. Is dat een bom — een torpedo - granaat — een mijn ?

Air-dropped "Short Invasion Phrasebook", autumn 1940

German	French	Dutch

4. Achtung! Englische E-Boote—Zerstörer—Kreuzer — Schlachtschiffe—Bomber !

5. Unser Schiff kentert — versinkt — brennt — explodiert!

6. Unsere Gruppe — unser Zug — unsere Kompanie — unse. Bataillon — unser Regiment geht unter !

7. Die Anderen — die ganze Division — das ganze Armeekorps auch !

8. Schon wieder geht eins unter !

9. Wo ist denn unsere Flotte — unsere Luftwaffe?

10. Hier riecht die See so nach Petroleum !

11. Hier brennt sogar das Wasser !

12. Schauen Sie, wie schön der Herr Hauptmann brennt !

13. Der Karl — der Willi — der Fritz — der Johann — der Abraham ist verkohlt — ertrunken — von den Schiffsschrauben zerfleischt.

14. Wir müssen umdrehen !

15. Wir fahren gegen Engelland!

---

4. Attention! ce sont des vedettes lance-torpilles — des contre-torpilleurs, des croiseurs des cuirassés — des bombardiers anglais !

5. Notre bateau chavire — coule — brûle — fait explosion !

6. Notre escouade — notre section — notre compagnie — notre bataillon — notre régiment est englouti (ou englouti?) !

7. Les autres — toute la division — tout le corps d'armée — l'est (ou le sont) aussi !

8. Un autre bateau est en train de couler.

9. Où est notre flotte — notre aviation?

10. La mer empeste le mazout, ici!

11. Même l'eau brûle ici !

12. Regarde comme notre capitaine brûle bien !

13. Charles — Guillaume — Frédérique — Jean — Abraham est carbonise — est noyé — est déchiqueté par les hélices.

14. Il faut faire demi-tour !

15. Nous partons pour l'Angleterre. (Tant pis pour vous !)

---

4. Pas op ! Britsche E-booten — torpedojagers — kruisers — slagschepen. — bommenwerpers !

5. Ons schip kapseist — zinkt — brandt — vliegt in de lucht !

6. Onze groep — afdeeling — compagnie-bataillon — regiment verdrinkt !

7. De anderen — de heele divisie — het geheele legercorps verdrinkt ook !

8. Daar zinkt weer een schip !

9. Waar is onze vloot — onze luchtmacht !

10. Wat stinkt de zee hier naar olie !

11. Hier staat waarachtig het water in brand!

12. Kijk eens hoe mooi de kapitein in brand staat !

13. Karel Willem Frits Johan — Abraham is verkoold — verdronken — tot pap gemalen door de schroeven van het schip.

14. We moeten omdraaien !

15. Wij varen gauw naar Engeland. (Arme bliksems !)

III. Nach der Invasion

1. Wir haben genug !

2. Sie sind noch immer im Lazarett.

3. Wo haben Sie sich den schönen Schnupfen — den Hexenschuss — die Lungenentzündung — den Nervenschock — geholt?

4. Mehr ist von uns nicht übrig geblieben.

5. Bitte, wo kann man hier die Totenlisten mal einsehen?

6. Wie sieht England eigentlich aus?

7. Es gab einmal eine deutsche Flotte.

8. Es gibt sehr viele englische Luftangriffe.

9. Wann findet die nächste Invasion statt?

10. Am 1., 15., 30. Januar, Februar, März, April, Mai, Juni, Juli, August, September, Oktober, November, Dezember — 1941, 1942, 1943, 1944, 1945 . . . usw.

11. nicht ! Du nicht ! Er nicht ! Wir nicht ! Sie auch nicht ! Aber Ihr vielleicht ?

12. Wir fahren gegen Engelland !

13. Wir wollen heim !

Zur Beachtung : Ein englischer Taschendolmetscher wird jedem deutschen Englandfahrer bei seiner Ankunft in einem englischen Kriegsgefangenenlager unentgeltlich ausgehändigt werden.

III. Après l'invasion

1. Nous en avons assez !

2. Ils sont encore à l'hôpital.

3. Où avez vous attrapé ce beau rhume — ce lumbago — cette pleurésie — cette commotion cérébrale?

4. Nous sommes les seuls qui nous nous en soyons tirés.

5. Où peut-on consulter la liste des tués et disparus, ici, s'il-vous-plaît?

6. Pouvez-vous me décrire l'Angleterre?

7. Il y avait une fois une flotte allemande.

8. Il y a un très grand nombre de raids anglais.

9. Quand la prochaine invasion doit-elle avoir lieu?

10. Elle doit avoir lieu le 1er, 15, 30 janvier, février, mars, avril, mai, juin, juillet, août, septembre, octobre, novembre, décembre — 1941, 1942, 1943, 1944, 1945, etc.

11. Pas moi ! Pas toi ! Pas lui ! Pas nous ! Pas eux ! Mais peut-être vous ?

12. Nous sommes partis pour l'Angleterre !

13. Nous voulons rentrer chez nous !

N.B. Un manuel de conversation en langue anglaise sera distribué gratuitement à chaque envahisseur lors de son arrivée au camp de prisonniers en Grande-Bretagne.

III. Na de invasie

1. Wij hebben er tabak van !

2. Zij liggen nog steeds in het hospitaal.

3. Waar heb je die mooie verkoudheid opgeloopen — spit — longontsteking — zenuwstoring ?

4. Dat's alles wat er van ons over is.

5. Kunt U mij ook zeggen waar ik de verlieslijsten kan makijken ?

6. Hoe ziet Engeland er eigenlijk uit?

7. Er was ereis een Duitsche vloot.

8. Er zijn veel Britsche luchtaanvallen.

9. Wanneer is de volgende invasie?

10. Op den 1 sten, 15 den, 30 sten Januari, Februari, Maart, April, Mei, Juni, Juli, Augustus, September, October, November, December — 1941, 1942, 1943, 1944, 1945, enzoovoorts.

11. Ik niet ! Jij niet ! Hij niet ! Wij niet ! Niemand van ons ! Misschien jij wel?

12. We wilden gauw naar Engeland !

13. Wij willen naar huis !

N.B. Iedere Duitsche reiziger naar Engeland krijgt een Engelsch zakwoordenboekje cadeau, zoodra hij in het krijgsgevangenkamp is aangekomen.

"Short Invasion Phrasebook"

teasing and derision' two or three times a week. In his second volume of autobiography, Black Boomerang (1962), Delmer records the transmission in early October of an amusing English lesson for would-be invaders. The script ran thus:

We English, as you know, are notoriously bad at languages, and so it will be best, meine Herren Engellandfahrer, if you learn a few useful English phrases before visiting us.

For your first lesson we will take: Die Kanaluberfahrt... the Channel crossing, the Chan-nel cros-sing. Now just repeat after me: Das Boot sinkt... the boat is sinking, the boat is sin-king. Das Wasser ist kalt... the water is cold. Sehr kalt... very cold.

Now, I will give you a verb that should come in useful. Again please repeat after me:

Ich brenne... I burn
Du brennst... you burn
Er brennt... he burns
Wir brennen... we burn
Ihr brennt... you are burning

Yes, meine Herren, in English, a rather practical language, we use the same word 'you' for both the singular and the plural:

Ihr brennt... you are burning
Sie brennen... they burn

And if I may be allowed to suggest a phrase: Der SS Sturmfuhrer brennt auch ganz schon... The SS captain is also burning quite nicely, the SS captain is al-so bur-ning quite nice-ly!

Delmer goes on to make a fascinating claim:

Crude stuff, but excellent in one important respect. The line about burning in the Channel fitted in perfectly, as of course it was intended to, with the information which our deception services had planted on Admiral Canaris, the head of Hitler's espionage. Our rumour agencies, too, had been busy spreading it everywhere. The mean murderous British, it was said, had apparatus in readiness with which they were going to set the Channel and the beaches on fire at such time as Hitler launched his boats. This was a lie. But it went over so well that it is believed by many Germans to this day.

The suggestion that Admiral Wilhelm Canaris, the chief of the German Abwehr intelligence service, was in some way party to the burning sea deception is unverifiable. Although Canaris was opposed to the Sealion plan for sound operational reasons, and is known to have passed limited information to the Allies later in the war via his mistress in Switzerland, the traffic is not thought to have been two-way. Yet Delmer's hint is mirrored in the German feature film Canaris, released in 1954, the plot of which is summarised in the following chapter. Although a film is hardly a reputable historical source, in this context it should be borne in mind that German testing of counter-measures against burning oil at Wilhelmshaven were staged on August 18th, a week before the first successful British sea flame barrage trial at Titchfield on August 24th. Was the considerable German research effort outlined in Chapter Two really the result of a lone German aircraft overflying the flawed trial at Dumpton on July 3rd? Perhaps. Or perhaps misinformation was indeed pipelined into the Abwehr by British intelligence through a covert conduit.

It can be asserted with rather more confidence that American intelligence chief Colonel William Donovan played an active role in spreading the burning sea rumour. Donovan, a millionaire Wall Street lawyer and an influential Republican, had worked with MI6 on an occasional basis since 1916, and wielded considerable political influence in Washington. British Security Co-ordination bureau chief William Stephenson established contact with Donovan immediately upon arriving in New York in June 1940, a link which paved the way for Donovan's visit to Britain the following month. His purpose was to assess the military situation first hand, and to counteract the gloomy reports sent back by Joseph Kennedy, America's defeatist ambassador in London. Donovan arrived on July 17th, and during the course of a remarkable tour lasting more than two weeks met the King, Churchill, the heads of MI6, MI5 and SOE, as well as other assorted senior intelligence figures including Desmond Morton and Beaumont-Nesbitt, and probably Hankey.

Neither Stephenson nor Donovan have been particularly well served by diligent biographers. However in Donovan of OSS, author Corey Ford claimed that:

Because he was Bill Donovan, the British showed him things no American had seen before: their top secret invention of radar, their newest interceptor planes, their coastal defences. He was made privy to some of Britain's ingenious propaganda devices, including the carefully planted rumour that

56

Stills from the 1954 film Canaris. After the German chief of intelligence examines the stolen film, he shows the general staff a model of a flame barrage at Hastings. Footage of 'bestial' British flame defences is then screened, and the invasion plan dismissed as suicidal. German countermeasures were tested a full week before the first successful British flame barrage test on August 24th 1940. Was the film less fantastical than it seemed? (Taurus Video)

a system of underwater pipelines could turn every beach and cove into a sea of flaming oil in case of German landings. They unlocked their safes, and initiated him into the mysteries of the SIS and the techniques of unorthodox warfare. He was particularly intrigued by their use of captured German spies as counter-agents and playbacks.

Given that no working sea flame barrages existed in late July 1940, it is unlikely that Donovan witnessed one in operation. Nevertheless both SOE and the PWD were already established in London, as was the PWD research station at Moody Down Farm. There is no reason to doubt that Donovan was briefed on their fiery work in progress, and its obvious propaganda potential, both black and white. Like his subordinate Robert Solborg, Donovan came to form a part of the clandestine pipeline by which the Big Lie of failed invasion was circulated worldwide.

In assessing the significance of Donovan's tour, intelligence historian Nigel West concludes that:

Wherever he went, he saw apparently well-equipped and well- armed troops preparing for an airborne invasion. The two fighter airfields he visited seemed to be in an advanced state of readiness to meet the Luftwaffe. Much of what Donovan saw was an elaborate deception to persuade him that Britain possessed the means to continue the fight. The King's performance had succeeded in convincing him of the nation's resolve; SIS's role was to persuade him that the country was logistically able to support its determination... Donovan's dramatic visit to England will remain one of the greatest intelligence triumphs of the war. On the basis of the opinions he expressed on his return, President Roosevelt agreed to enter into Lend-Lease negotiations with Britain which resulted in the delivery of desperately-needed equipment.

In this way, the myth of invasion engaged and repulsed became the first significant British propaganda victory of the Second World War. As John Baker White later offered:

The burning sea story was our first large-scale attempt at a Big Lie, and it proved amazingly successful. It was produced by people who were still amateurs at the game, and projected through a machine still far from complete. But it worked.

Just how successful, and how remarkably deathless, is examined in the following chapter.

'LIKE FISH IN A FRYING PAN'
The Burning Sea Myth 1940-1957

On November 1st 1940 The War Illustrated ran a lengthy feature which set the pattern for much subsequent coverage of the mid-September mystery. Accompanied by a news agency photograph of smiling German invasion troops on board a minesweeper, the piece purported to present an account of the 'completest rout so far.' The text is significant in that it marries together almost all the black rumours concerning failed invasion fed into the pipeline by British intelligence agencies up to that point, but now with the added dimension of burning seas.

What happened on September 16th? Nothing less, it now seems probable, than an attempted invasion of England... At the time there were many stories in circulation concerning the supposed invasion attempt, and the English newspapers were full of accounts of smashing blows delivered at Hitler's barges assembled in the invasion bases; on that same Sunday night the RAF bombers left their mark on Hamburg and Wilhelmshaven, on Antwerp, Flushing and Ostend, on Dunkirk, Calais, Boulogne and Le Havre.

A few days later some of the American papers were far more communicative. They did not hint at an invasion attempt; rather they stated in the most definite terms that the armada of invasion had actually sailed. Thus the New York Sun stated that the barges - 'very light, of wood and metal, and obviously intended solely for a one-way trip' - each contained 200 Germans will full equipment. 'Evidently the Germans had counted on their airmen being able to silence the land batteries before these were able to annihilate the invaders, who were helpless because they did not carry artillery... They sank under a withering fire as soon as they appeared. Meanwhile, detachments of the British Fleet appeared to the rear cutting off the barges from France.'

The carnage was reported to have been terrific; neutral observers stated that the number of killed, drowned and wounded were to be counted in tens of thousands. All available hospital accommodation in and around the Channel ports had to be commandeered for the German wounded, and one report quoted a French doctor who said he had seen several thousand severely burned German soldiers in hospitals in occupied France; they had been, said the doctor, on board transports and barges preparing for the invasion of

England when they were caught by British oil bombs, and the flaming oil on the surface of the water burned the troops as they leapt into the sea.

Many stories were current, too, in the south of England concerning large numbers of dead Germans who, so it was said, has been washed ashore in several places. There were tales of closed lorries going to and from the beach at one point, of mysterious ambulances moving through the night; nor was there any doubt that some dead Germans had actually been washed up, but it was officially stated that these were Nazi airmen whose 'planes had been shot down into the sea. Perhaps more to the point were the many stories published in American papers of large numbers of German dead being washed ashore in the neighbourhood of the invasion ports, particularly on the beaches near Le Havre, Calais and Boulogne.

By way of explanation of these American reports and English rumours, responsible quarters in London expressed the opinion that a considerable proportion of the German divisions detailed for the invasion of England had actually embarked, when the fleet of flat-bottomed barges was caught by the bombers of the RAF, whose bombardment was so effective that the enemy fleet was obliged to put to sea, and lay a short distance from the French coast. Then rising winds compelled the vessels to return to their ports; and the French people who had seen their departure and witnessed their return, concluded that the invasion had been attempted and had been driven back. Yet another explanation was that the RAF bombers had caught the invasion fleet during a rehearsal... It was a fitting end to the day which Hitler had chosen to be Der Tag.

Fitting, perhaps, but also fictional. More than any other invasion myth of 1940, however, it was the claim that the British had fired the sea which came to preoccupy minds worldwide. In the United States, the New York Times fanned the flames still further by printing an even more fantastical report six weeks later, on December 15th, in which oil bombs and torpedoes were displaced by undersea fuel tanks. Its author, Boris Nikolayevsky, was described as 'a distinguished Russian publicist and historian' resident in France before his recent arrival in New York, with 'particularly close contacts with French political circles.' The report was syndicated across several titles owned by the North American Newspaper Alliance, and appeared beneath the lengthy headline NAZI INVADERS HELD 'CONSUMED BY FIRE' - DEAD ARE PUT AT 80,000:

There have been at least two attempts by the Germans to invade England from the French coast, and in both instances the Nazis were literally consumed by fire. This was the story told in France by workers from the occupied area along the Channel coast and confirmed by nurses who worked in hospitals attending German soldiers who had escaped from the British flames.

The first invasion attempt was made in August, the second early in September. Both failed when British planes dropped incendiary bombs and set afire tanks of oil and gasoline in the Channel. As disclosed by Frenchmen in a position to know, the British sowed the Channel with oil tanks sufficiently beneath the surface to be hidden from view. Parallel with these the British anchored thousands of gasoline tanks. Then they waited for the Germans.

On the first occasion the Germans advanced in approximately 1200 specially constructed aluminum barges, each bearing about 50 soldiers and equipment. They struck the oil and gasoline line about midway between the French and British coasts. At the same time British planes in the skies began raining incendiary bombs. In a few minutes the Channel was a mass of fire enveloping the Nazi barges.

CASUALTIES SAID TO BE HIGH: 'We were caught like fish in a frying pan,' was the way a German soldier who escaped from the debacle described it to a French nurse. Only a few thousand Germans succeeded in reaching the French coast. The others perished in the sea or were burned to death. The Germans tried again in September, over another route, and suffered a similar fate. People in the occupied French ports estimate that perhaps as many as 80,000 German troops perished in the two attempts. The fact is that hospitals in occupied France are filled with Nazi soldiers, all of them suffering from severe burns. Thousands of dead Germans have been washed ashore.

According to reports brought back by persons who succeeded in making their way to the unoccupied zone, there was a wave of mutinies in the German Army in September, many of the troops declaring that they would not face again the 'burning sea' when they learned that a third attempt at invasion of England was being planned.

If Boris Nikolayevsky existed at all, it is possible that his article was the work of another White Russian emigre lately arrived from France, Robert Solborg, and channelled via Intrepid. Although in Britain the censor still forbade publication of invasion reports, Nikolayevsky's story was repeated in the Daily Telegraph on December 16th. It is therefore hardly surprising that Rear-Admiral Thomson was moved to record in 1947 that:

> In the whole course of the war there was no story which gave me so much trouble as this one of the attempted German invasion, flaming oil and 30,000 burned Germans.

Quite why British intelligence sources continued to promote the failed invasion myth as late as December 1940 remains unclear, although by then in Britain the rumour had moved beyond Thomson's control. In early 1941 several British publications perpetuated the catastrophe myth, among them an HMSO pamphlet titled Bomber Command, and the January edition of the popular aviation magazine the Aeroplane, which described a landing 'repelled in disorder with heavy losses' on September 16th. Later an official statement issued through the Ministry of Information by the Free French Information Service referred to '30,000 Germans drowning in an attempted embarkation last September', although according to Thomson British editors were asked to give the rogue paragraph no publicity.

Most obeyed, and as a result it was a book by James Spaight, The Battle of Britain 1940, published later in 1941, which did much to keep alive the invasion myth. In yet another speculative account distilled from earlier press reports, Spaight implied that the sea had been fired accidentally:

> In mid-September something happened which is still a mystery. There were persistent rumours then that an invasion was attempted and was foiled by our naval forces. That was probably untrue, but it is fairly certain that some kind of disaster did overtake the 'invasion fleet' at that time. It is known that a large number of German soldiers had to be treated in hospital for burns, the result, it was reported, of a heavy raid by the Royal Air Force at that time. The raid caught the troops just when they were engaged in a 'dress rehearsal' for embarkation; the boats in which they were carried were sunk and when they took to the water the oil, set alight by the incendiary bombs, burned them severely before they could be rescued. For days after this incident bodies of dead soldiers were being washed up on the French, Belgian and Dutch coasts. A bad storm contributed to the German losses of boats and men at about the same date.

In his 'Summary and Conclusion' Spaight drove his point home:

One particular series of raids was especially damaging. It is believed to have caught the German soldiers and sailors just at the moment when a kind of 'dress rehearsal' was being staged and to have resulted in the killing and wounding of thousands of the troops embarked. There were certainly heavy demands on hospital accommodation in occupied France just about that time, in mid-September. Bodies of uniformed Germans continued to be washed up on our shores for some days after that date.

The burning sea legend was heavily endorsed by the publication of two more celebrated books in 1941: Berlin Diary by William Shirer, and Under The Iron Heel by Lars Moen. Both were by American authors, and both appeared in British and American editions. As detailed in Chapter Five, while in Geneva on September 16th 1940 Shirer claimed to have heard rumours that:

Either in attempted German raids with sizeable landing parties on the English coast, or in rehearsals with boats and barges off the French coast, the British had given the Germans a bad pummelling. The British used a new type of wireless-directed torpedo which ignited oil on the water and burned the barges.

A still more vivid picture was painted by Lars Moen in Under The Iron Heel. By his own account, this former newsman and screenwriter had been working for a Belgian film manufacturer, and found himself overtaken by the German offensive in May 1940. Moen remained in Antwerp until October 22nd, when he left to return to America. His book, tagged 'an American reports on occupied Europe', appeared in the States early the following year, and was published - unabridged - in Britain in September 1941. Sales were brisk, for according to Moen:

On or about September 16th, a considerable force of towed triple-barges set out from a point along the Belgian coast, constituting the first wave of the attack, which was to occupy a strip on the English coast at which liners could put in and disembark the invasion troops. At a point probably not far from the Belgian coast, they were spotted by the British. Destroyers of the Royal Navy then managed to cut them off, and forced them well out into the North Sea. Here planes of the RAF dropped oil drums with great quantities of oil on and near the barges, then followed with incendiary bombs which turned the whole into a blazing inferno.

During the first weeks of October, the bodies of hundreds of German soldiers were being washed ashore along the Belgian coast, especially in the vicinity of Ostend. Many of them were so badly burned as to be almost unrecognisable. Many of the invasion barges were missing, although the naval craft and merchant liners were still in the harbour, their number having been increased by fresh arrivals.

None of these facts, taken alone, could be taken as proof that an attempted invasion actually took place. Taken collectively, they all point in one direction. I believe these facts to be exact. I first learned of the burned patients from a Belgian nurse working in an Antwerp hospital; Americans living near Ostend confirmed reports of the bodies being washed ashore. Later, I heard these stories scores of times, which proves nothing - but it was extremely significant that reports from the most widely scattered sources were unanimous on one point: that a considerable number of German soldiers had been badly burned.

Apocryphal Belgian and French nurses would come to form part of the very fabric of the myth, as discussed elsewhere in this chapter. As Moen freely admitted, his account was strung together from rumours heard first in Belgium and Lisbon, and then on board the liner Exeter during his repatriation to the United States in October. It will be recalled that Robert Solborg had returned to New York on the very same American Export Line vessel one month before.

Later, en route to Lisbon, in Lisbon and on board the Exeter, I had the opportunity to compare notes with persons coming from other invasion ports and from England, and putting together all of the corroborative evidence, it seems to me an overwhelming probability that the following took place...

In truth, Moen's version of the mid-September mystery bears an uncomfortably close resemblance to the story published by the New York Sun, and to the Nikolayevsky account from the New York Times. It can safely be discounted, although Moen himself appears simply to have been gullible rather than dishonest. Unlike Moen, William Shirer eventually concluded that reports of 'an actual full-fledged' invasion attempt were without foundation. Certainly in Britain no record exists of any wireless-directed petroleum torpedo, or of an RAF operation in which fuel drums were dropped into the Channel. Indeed no submarine or bomber then in service was capable of carrying a payload of oil sufficient to kill 80 men, let alone 80,000. Nikolayevsky's moored gasoline tanks were similarly fictitious, with all three variants revealing the end that the

Petroleum Warfare Department had in mind, but - tellingly - not the actual means. Nonetheless, Shirer's widely-read Berlin Diary added a further layer of plausibility to the story. For on returning to Berlin from Geneva, Shirer witnessed scenes on September 18th and 19th 1940 which have never been satisfactorily explained:

September 18th: We arrived at the Potsdamer Bahnhof right on time... I noticed several lightly wounded soldiers, mostly airmen, getting off a special car which had been attached to our train. From their bandages their wounds looked like burns. I noticed also the longest Red Cross train I've ever seen. It stretched from the station for half a mile to beyond the bridge over the Landwehr Canal. Orderlies were swabbing it out, the wounded having been unloaded, probably, during the night. The Germans usually unload their hospital trains after dark so that the populace will not be unduly disturbed by one of the grimmer sides of glorious war. I wondered where so many wounded could have come from as the armies in the west stopped fighting three months ago. As there were only a few porters I had to wait some time on the platform and picked up a conversation with a railway workman. He said most of the men taken from the hospital train were suffering from burns. Can it be that the tales I heard in Geneva had some truth in them after all?

Shirer concluded that the mysterious bandaged figures warranted further investigation. The very next day he recorded:

September 19th: Returning to town we noticed a large crowd standing on a bridge which spanned a railroad line. We thought there had been an accident. But we found the people staring silently at a long Red Cross train unloading wounded. This is getting interesting. Only during the fortnight in September when the Poles were being crushed and a month this spring when the west was being annihilated have we seen so many hospital trains in Berlin. A diplomat told me this morning his legation had checked two other big hospital trains unloading wounded in the Charlottenburg railroad yards yesterday. This makes four long trains of wounded in the last two days that I know have arrived here.

Shirer's account is not easily dismissed, although precisely what he witnessed first-hand beyond 'several...airmen' seems ambiguous. The diarist later concluded that the men in Berlin were casualties of an exercise caught by the RAF, but Shirer was actively pro-British, as revealed by the official BSC war history, and the suspicion remains that in 1941 he 'wrote up' the hospital train story as a morale booster, at a time when the war was going particularly badly for Britain. There exist several reports of similar trains at the Gare du Nord in Brussels, and even the landing of a bedraggled German party in Antwerp docks. Yet surely even the most unreconstructed conspiracy theorist will baulk at the notion that, since 1945, all mention of a large- scale amphibious operation, which resulted in trainloads of German casualties, can have been expunged from every memoir, history and official file.

In 1941 Thomson issued another edict forbidding all submissions for the home press or agencies, or for broadcast, 'indicating or inferring an attempted enemy invasion of this country.' Evidently the censor had no control over public lectures, however, for on April 7th 1942 a jobbing American journalist named Charles M Barbe gave a talk titled 'None So Blind' to a small London audience at the Royal Institute of International Affairs. Barbe, a man of many parts, was a former musician who had volunteered as an ambulance driver early in 1940, and saw service in France. The text of his talk included the following paragraphs:

Along with a few others who did not feel like the show was over I stayed on in Paris, and during the last part of August this curiosity I speak of got the better of me again, and along with another chap - a Frenchman, believe it or not, who felt an equal curiosity - we had been hearing stories of something which was going to happen round the 15th of September, during the first, second or third week in September. So we went up into the military zone, which was something I would not do again.

From about the 10th to the 16th September we were in a small house about ten kilometres south of Dunkirk, a good healthy stone's throw from the Channel, during what is commonly termed the Battle of Britain. Maybe you remember it. Now I have broadcast several times for the BBC since I have been in London and I have written the story of what we saw happen there and what I was able to confirm later on in Paris and Berlin, but it has always been cut out of my scripts. I understand that I might be able to mention it here. Anyway I'll take a chance. The 161st and 197th Schleswig-Holstein SS divisions and the 67th Hessian Division, three of the prime, crack SS divisions, never bothered anyone after the 15th September. The better part of 33,000 men started out from the shores of France, and not one of them ever got back to the shores of France alive.

I do not know what happened. About the 17th or 18th September on our way back to Paris we saw something strange... at a point on the coast quite near to

Dieppe, we saw bodies on the shore like driftwood, something which could in some cases be identified as once having been human, while others looked like blackened tree stumps, and I don't believe I shall ever get the stench out of my nose, not if I live to be 1000 years old. They were just burned beyond recognition. I had previously spoken to a couple of German soldiers just north of Paris, who had told me that they had been badly burned during the latter part of August. One of the boys said he would be shot before he went back. He said he was out in a rowing boat, fishing, that is the official word, fishing, when, in his words, the sea exploded in flames. As I say, I do not know what happened. I only know what the results were.

Barbe went on to explain that None So Blind was the title of an abortive book project based on his experiences in Occupied France:

I had thoroughly determined when I came to England to be unique among journalists in that I was not going to write a book; but I had been in England less than two weeks when a book was talked over as a sequel to Berlin Diary by one of England's better publishers. So I wrote about 40 to 50,000 words of it and then submitted it to a gentleman who looked it over and the replied in a couple of days that he was sorry, he had gone over it with a couple of his directors and had found that he could not publish it because it would not help the war effort. That was alright with me, but it was very much along the lines of the way I have been talking today. Perhaps that was why it would not help the war effort.

None So Blind never was published, and the lecture failed in its presumed purpose to excite fresh interest from London editors. In truth, and like Lars Moen before him, Barbe was simply an adventurer - musician, ambulance driver, journalist - keen to enhance his reputation at the expense of truth and integrity. Certainly the few purported facts contained in his account suggest a highly unreliable witness. Chief among these is his identification of three SS divisions which never existed, and whose given names bear no resemblance to any units raised before or during the Second World War. While it is true that accredited American correspondents such as Shirer were afforded brief supervised visits to the invasion coast in France and Belgium, it is unlikely that any were given the free reign implied by Barbe.

His lecture did not escape the attention of the censor. According to Thomson:

An American broadcaster, who was one of our many visitors from the United States in those days, evidently believed that Chatham House was an excellent place to make a name for himself in London and that his audience wouldn't examine too closely the accuracy of his statements. He certainly made a most moving speech. As an American correspondent accredited to the German Forces in 1940, he had, he said, been on the French coast just after the abortive attempt at invasion. He described the floating bodies, the interviews he had with survivors in hospital, and made some of his hearers turn pale with his references to the smell of charred flesh which hung all along the coast. Nobody, however, got up and suggested he was economising in accuracy. Nor would it have been wise for anyone to have done so even if he had known the facts. For we were not discouraging the circulation of this rumour in Germany. It was even contained in pamphlet dropped over Germany by the RAF.

Here Thomson is himself guilty of legend ostentation, for Barbe made no mention of hospital visits. However his lecture offers an insight into the particular problem posed by loquacious American commentators. Although in reality the voluntary code imposed by Thomson's office had almost mandatory effect, the censor had no jurisdiction over foreign nationals or their employers. The likes of Barbe, talking loosely at Chatham House, could not be gagged, as Thomson admitted:

Our greatest handicaps in the case of these 'non-security' bans were the friendly neutrals. Influential visitors from the USA - including well known American newspaper proprietors and correspondents, and broadcasters, came over to this country in an unending stream from the autumn of 1940 until the end of the war. Before they went back to America, we would tell them what we were banning from publication in this country and would examine any documents they were taking back with them. This was done on the basis of giving them friendly advice and on the unquestionably correct assumption that they wouldn't want to do anything to help the Nazis.

Nonetheless, when they felt that what we were banning was somewhat far-fetched, they very naturally used their own discretion when they got back to the USA and made things rather awkward for me, in my dealings with British editors, by broadcasting or writing about a forbidden subject, such as parachute mines. Ralph Ingersoll did so freely in a book and I found it difficult to prevent our press making quotations from it.

Following Barbe's lecture at Chatham House in April 1942, the mid-September mystery largely vanished from the pages of the press until October 1944.

In the interim, fact and fiction began to blur. As early as 1940 the author Graham Greene, himself an MI6 officer, published a short story called The Lieutenant Died Last. The plot revolved around 'an unrecorded victory in 1940' in the village of Potter, during which a detachment of German parachute troops are swiftly bagged by a lone poacher, thus providing 'a discouraging failure for the German High Command.' Greene later developed on this theme in his superior screenplay for the film Went The Day Well?, which proved a notable commercial success on release in November 1942, and which lent Jack Higgins inspiration for his runaway 1975 bestseller The Eagle Has Landed. A very similar novel, When The Bells Rang, was published anonymously in May 1943. The plot turned on a German landing in April 1941, during which the Kentish village of Russocks is occupied by jackbooted Nazi thugs. Neither Green nor the author of When the Bells Rang made any reference to floating corpses or flaming oil, although the popular Will Hay comedy feature The Goose Steps Out (1942) contains a pointed reference to visiting Germans receiving the 'warmest welcome' of their lives, apparently a nod to the burning sea rumour two years earlier.

By 1943 the invasion legend had lodged so deeply in the British psyche that questions were raised in the House of Commons. On July 29th 1943 the robust Conservative member for West Leeds, Major Vyvyan Adams, enquired whether:

As questions of security can, at this distance in time, no longer be involved, will [the government] describe the character and extent of any attempt at the invasion of these islands made by the enemy during the summer and early autumn of 1940?

Clement Attlee, then Lord President, sidestepped the question:

It is well known throughout the world that the enemy's preparations for invasion in 1940 were frustrated by the Royal Air Force. As, however, the staffs of the Service Departments are at the present time heavily engaged on current duties, my right honourable friend the Prime Minister is reluctant to impose on them the additional work of preparing a detailed answer which would satisfy my honourable and gallant friend's curiosity without at the same time disclosing to the enemy the extent of our sources of information.

A brief exchange followed, during which Adams derided the answer, and was in turn accused of impudence. Eleven months later, on June 20th 1944, Adams returned to the matter and demanded that Churchill now indicate 'in broad terms' the nature and scale of any invasion attempt in 1940. Again, the reply did little to satisfy his curiosity:

MR CHURCHILL: I have nothing which I can usefully add at this stage to the reply which my right honourable friend the Lord President of the Council gave to my honourable and gallant friend on 29th July last.

MAJOR ADAMS: May I ask my right honourable friend if he cannot tell at this interval of time, as a matter of historical interest, whether the enemy ever set in motion the apparatus of a sea-borne invasion?

MR CHURCHILL: Well, Sir, it is a matter on which I should not like to take people off other current jobs in order to use their time today. I do not know what my honourable and gallant friend means by 'set in motion'. 'Set in motion', in the sense of crossing the Channel, no; 'set in motion', in the sense of making very heavy concentrations, both of troops and ships, to cross the Channel, yes.

MR SHINWELL: Can the right honourable gentleman say that, if such an attempt was made, at any rate, was it unsuccessful?

MR CHURCHILL: Yes, sir.

MAJOR ADAMS: Can my right honourable friend add this - did any of that shipping emerge from the ports across the Channel?

MR CHURCHILL: Not to my belief. A great deal of it was smashed in the ports and then they changed their minds.

The Major clearly suspected that a landing had been attempted, and although the written record in Hansard made no mention of fire or corpses, Adams' questions reflected (and no doubt fed) public interest in the unsolved riddle. By the time the member for West Leeds raised the issue in Parliament the original bodies legend had been blurred with the later burning sea rumour, so that the countless corpses supposedly washed ashore in 1940 were now usually described as burned or charred. Typical of this blurring is The Lion Roared Its Defiance, a privately-printed Suffolk Home Guard memoir produced in 1944, which recalled of September 15th 1940 that 'charred bodies of German soldiers were washed to the southern and eastern shores', adding darkly that 'the events of that night may never be fully disclosed.'

Others were equally keen to debunk the story. Following the great heroism of the celebrated raid on the Ruhr dams by 617 Squadron in May 1943, Squadron Leader Guy Gibson was commissioned to write an account that would describe in realistic fashion the work of aircrew in both Fighter and Bomber Command. Gibson was killed over Holland in September 1944, and his ghost-written memoir, Enemy Coast Ahead, not published until 1946. Discussing the Battle of the Barges in September 1940, Gibson quoted from Berlin Diary by William Shirer to support his contention that Bomber Command had rendered the invasion ports all but unusable. Where one aspect of the invasion summer was concerned, however, Gibson begged to differ with the American:

There were rumours that they actually had moved out and that we had sunk them. There were rumours that thousands of German soldiers were buried on the east coast of England, soldiers who had been hit by Bomber Command, who had drowned and washed ashore. These rumours were untrue, and no-one in this country will even know anyone who saw a dead German soldier, although many a man will claim to know someone who knows someone else who buried one.

Yet Gibson's claim is demonstrably false, if only because the recovery of the body of Heinrich Poncke at Littlestone on October 20th 1940. A comparable mass-market account was provided by an equally celebrated war veteran in 1952, when novelist Evelyn Waugh published the first part of his masterful trilogy Sword of Honour. Although Men at Arms is a work of fiction, the book closely mirrors Waugh's own early war service in the Royal Marines. In September 1940 Waugh took part in the ill-fated expedition to Dakar, and in his later fictional version notes through his protagonist Guy Crouchback:

Wireless news from England was full of air raids. Some of the men were consumed with anxiety; most were consoled by a rumour, quite baseless, which was travelling the whole world in an untraceable manner, that the invasion had sailed and been defeated, that the whole Channel was full of charred German corpses.

In August 1944 the existence of the Petroleum Warfare Department was revealed to the public for the first time, at a press conference staged by Geoffrey Lloyd at Moody Down Farm. Various anti-invasion weapons were demonstrated to journalists, and footage released for use in newsreels. Typical is the report published the following day in the Daily Express:

A man in a bowler hat, it was disclosed last night, headed a committee which has produced Britain's newest secret weapon, the flame thrower, which is now helping the British and Canadian forces to burn their way through France. That man has been known to those who still run cars as the man responsible for their petrol allowances - Mr Geoffrey Lloyd, Petroleum Minister...

But since 1940 he has had another job as well, a secret job. He has been head of what is now revealed as the Petroleum Warfare Department, created to produce stop-gap anti-invasion weapons based on burning oil. He stated: 'All this has developed from our first crude experiments to improvise burning oil defences on the beach at Ramsgate on a June afternoon in 1940. All of us who were there became keen believers in the effectiveness of flame warfare. That band grew, and included people with the most varied and, indeed, unorthodox qualifications.'

During the second half of 1944 the rapid Allied advance across Europe brought troops and journalists into contact with liberated civilians, when the comments of some served to revive interest in the catastrophe myth. WA Birkbeck, who took part in the liberation of Antwerp in September 1944, recalled:

While we were enjoying the gaiety and celebrations a friend and I were invited to take tea with an old Londoner who had married a Belgian soldier after the First World War. Their daughter was a nurse in an Antwerp hospital. During our walk around the district watching collaborators tried, the nurse remarked, 'the best thing you ever did was set the sea on fire.' I asked when it was that we set the sea on fire, to which she replied 1940, and that, 'I know because I was on duty in the hospital. The British set the sea on fire, and they were all so terribly burned.'

After speaking with another nurse in Brussels, a British United Press correspondent named John Parris claimed to have uncovered 'final details' of 'Hitler's calamitous attempt to invade Britain on September 16th 1940.' The News of the World ran the story on October 1st 1944:

Thousands of German soldiers - 50,000 so it is said - were burned to death or maimed for life on that September day. 'A nightmare in hell' was how German soldiers described it after the RAF, catching the Nazi fleet in mid-Channel, dumped oil on the water and set fire to it with incendiary bullets.

Belgians with whom I talked were surprised to learn that the British people had never been fully told of the attempt, which appeared to be common knowledge in Belgium. I heard one side of the story from Renee Meurisse, a Belgian Red Cross Nurse, in charge of a group of refugees at the time.

'During September 17th,' Renee told me, 'we heard rumours that thousands of bodies of German soldiers were being washed ashore along the Belgian beaches. At seven o'clock that night a German Red Cross train of 40 coaches pulled into Brussels Station. We had been expecting a refugee train, so we were surprised when we saw a train-load of Germans. The commandant, tired and in crumpled uniform, approached me and asked if we could help his wounded. He said that the train had been shunted on to the wrong line, and his men were dying for lack of treatment. We agreed to help, sent a call for more nurses and ambulances, and began taking the wounded from the train. The moans and screams were terrible.'

'I personally helped to carry a young German soldier from the train. He was horribly burned about the head and shoulders. A doctor assisted me to put him in a corner, and we determined to find out, if we could, exactly what had happened to him. We began by inquiring about his mother and sweetheart, and after each answer I would ask, "Where were you going and what happened?" Finally we managed to piece the story together.'

'He said they had been told they were going to invade Britain, that nothing was going to stop them, that it was just a matter of getting into boats and crossing the Channel. He told me: "It was horrible. The sea was ablaze. the British they bombed and machine-gunned us. Hell couldn't be worse." Then he died, there on the stretcher. We looked after more than 500 soldiers as best we could. many of them died in Brussels railway station, others in our hospitals.'

Renee explained that other nurses told her more stories they had picked up from German soldiers. "Thousands of us started out and we expected to be in England tonight," they said. For days afterwards the bodies of German soldiers, their heads and shoulders burned, were washed ashore, and it was impossible for the Nazis to preserve the secret any longer. 'The German Red Cross trains passed through Brussels for three days,' Renee went on. 'We asked for a supply of medical equipment for the Germans, but they didn't have much.'

The arrival of at least one hospital train at the Gare du Nord in September 1940 was confirmed by Agnes Mann, then a schoolgirl in Brussels. However, while the story told by Meurisse might conceivably tie in with the hospital trains seen by Shirer in Berlin, firm conclusions are difficult to draw. The official history of the German army medical service does not record large- scale casualties caused by burning in September 1940, while enquiries placed by the author with the Bundesarchiv drew a similar blank. Postwar research by Sealion historian Walter Ansell indicated that testing of flame countermeasures produced no 'noteworthy casualties', having canvassed senior German naval personnel directly involved in the operational planning. In 1957 BBC researchers placed press adverts in French and Belgian newspapers appealing for eyewitnesses to the failed invasion, or its aftermath. None came forward with hard evidence. In conclusion, if trains carrying up to 500 casualties each continued to arrive in Brussels for three days, it beggars belief that no German servicemen have come forward since 1945 to tell or sell the story of disaster on the scale of the Dieppe raid.

Nonetheless, equally colourful reports continued to surface closer to home. In May 1945 a Daily Express journalist met one man who claimed to have watched the invasion gambit 'one quiet weekend' in September 1940 from a spot on the Sussex coast near Bognor Regis.

He told of coastal guns going in action against a fleet of German invasion barges, of RAF bombers roaring overhead, of hundreds of uniformed bodies being washed up on the shores. 'And there were other whispers in this country: "Jerry has tried it, you know... all wiped out... burning oil."

In 1945 Geoffrey Lloyd became Minister of Information, and on June 3rd devoted his first press conference to revealing more precise details of the various petroleum weapons devised for the defence of Britain 1940. Copies of the air-delivered leaflet Short Invasion Phrasebook were distributed, as well as stills of mobile flamethrowers in action at Newhaven harbour. His press call made front pages on both sides of the Atlantic, largely because Lloyd admitted for the first time that British intelligence agencies had fostered the burning sea rumour overseas.

It always seemed to happen that when we were conducting full-scale experiments and making a tremendous blaze there was a German aeroplane about. On many occasions it came and bombed us. In this way the Germans must have known what we were doing, and in fact they showed us they expected us to use flames as a defence, for they carried out experiments with asbestos suits. But there was some defect in the helmets used and their own men got badly burned about the face. This gave rise to a rumour that an invasion had been attempted, and when we heard of it we used it to the full. Leaflets were dropped in France assuring the German soldiers that there was a warm reception awaiting them should they attempt invasion.

Describing the mid-September mystery as the 'biggest secret' of the war, the Daily Express also reprised their coverage of the anonymous Bognor native and Renee Meurisse, the Belgian nurse. From the account printed in the Daily Telegraph, the following may be added to Lloyd's disclosures:

We on this side, by leaflets and other means, let the German troops on the French coast know about the inferno awaiting them if they tried to invade us. There is evidence that the whole thing had a great morale effect on them. But it was not true that they ever tried an invasion. I am told that they had ordered 100,000 asbestos suits but apparently their experiments were abandoned.

Wisely separating fact from fiction, the New York Times offered a more balanced opinion:

History does not turn on so simple a matter as an asbestos uniform that will not keep out fire. Britain was saved by valiant leadership and the unconquerable spirit of her people. The petroleum defence worked out by Mr Lloyd, Lord Hankey and others may have saved the world years of bloodshed and suffering.

On November 18th 1946 the myth and reality of 1940 was again addressed in the House of Commons, now under Labour management. On this occasion the subject was raised by two Conservative backbenchers, Wing Commander Norman Hulbert and Sir Hugh Lucas-Tooth. Having fielded Major Adams' questions in 1943 and 1944, Clement Attlee (by now Prime Minister) was already well versed on the subject, although his written reply was drafted by the War Office. Following a brief resume of the Sealion operational plan, and of British defence strategy, it was stated that:

(11) It has been widely believed in this country that a German invasion attempt was actually launched in 1940. This belief is based partly on the fact that a number of German bodies were washed up on the south coast of England in August and September 1940; and partly on the knowledge that the 'invasion imminent' signal was issued by General Headquarters, Home

Forces on 7th September. The facts are as stated in the following paragraphs...

(12) In August 1940, the Germans were embarking their army in the barges in harbours along the French coast, but there is no evidence that they ever left harbour as a fleet to invade this country. Bombing raids on those harbours were carried out by Bomber Command and some barges which put to sea, probably to escape the raids, were sunk either by bombing or on encountering bad weather. During the next six weeks bodies of German soldiers were washed up at scattered points along the coast between Cornwall and Yarmouth (amounting to about 36 over a period of a month).

Although some might demur, there seems little reason to doubt that this figure is accurate. Certainly 'about 36' in the course of one month is more plausible than anything between 30,000 or 80,000. Although Poncke alone can be identified with any certainty, William Robinson's account provides further evidence in support. Three years later Churchill himself endorsed the War Office estimate. In Their Finest Hour, the second volume of his lengthy and rather subjective war history, Churchill repeated the substance of the Commons statement made in 1946, while at the same time adding a little embroidery of his own:

During August the corpses of about 40 German soldiers were washed up at scattered points along the coast between the Isle of Wight and Cornwall. The Germans had been practising embarkations in the barges along the French coast. Some of these barges put out to sea on order to escape British bombing and were sunk, either by bombing or bad weather. This was the source of a widespread rumour that the Germans had attempted an invasion and had suffered very heavy losses either by drowning or by being burnt in patches of sea covered with flaming oil. We took no steps to contradict such tales, which spread freely through the occupied countries in a wildly exaggerated form and gave much encouragement to the oppressed populations. In Brussels, for instance, a shop exhibited men's bathing suits marked 'For Channel Swimming.'

The bathing costumes were, of course, cut from whole cloth woven by British intelligence, while Churchill muddled timing, and managed to confuse Great Yarmouth in Norfolk with the smaller Yarmouth on the Isle of Wight. Despite these flaws, Churchill's brief mention came to be accepted as the definitive account of the catastrophe myth for almost a decade. For although Flame Over

Britain (Banks), Blue Pencil Admiral (Thomson) and The Big Lie (Baker White) had appeared in 1946, 1947 and 1955 respectively, none sold in large quantities, and were all but ignored by subsequent historians.

In Germany the failed invasion rumour was also deeply entrenched, and given new currency in 1954 with the release of Canaris, a superior monochrome feature directed by Alfred Weidenmann. The film offered up a liberal account of the career of Admiral Wilhelm Canaris, the German chief of intelligence who acted, albeit sporadically, as an Allied informant. During scenes concerned with Operation Sealion in 1940, an Abwehr agent effortlessly removes a canister of secret film from a Whitehall office, which in Berlin is found to contain graphic evidence of flame throwers, Fougasses and coastal flame barrages. The film is genuine PWD footage shot at Studland Bay and Moody Down Farm in 1941, and a detailed scale model of a fictional flame barrage installation at Hastings is also unveiled. Canaris has only to exhibit these several 'beast eating' devices to the German High Command to secure the cancellation of Sealion as 'suicidal.'

In a letter to the author in 1992, Weidenmann claimed that the PWD footage used in the film had been discovered in a Paris archive. He could shed no light on why screenwriter Erich Ebermeyer (who died in 1970) had attached such significance to the role of flame warfare in foiling Sealion, although Herbert Reinecker, who worked on the shooting script, offered the oblique observation that 'history is like a tart - it chases the man who pays most.' Little credibility attaches to subsequent accounts of an actual landing, such as that published by one 'Konrad Burg' in Landser magazine. This tale of a thwarted Waffen SS raid on the east coast of England may in turn have inspired the opening chapter of Death's Head, a pulp novel by Leo Kessler published in 1972. The charred body myth later inspired another fictional work, Sea Wrack, written by Raymond Hitchcock in 1980.

In 1957 a more serious attempt to uncover the truth was made by Peter Fleming in his book Invasion 1940. A wartime member of both MI(R) and SOE, Fleming had been responsible for co-ordinating Home Guard Auxiliary Units during the invasion summer of 1940. His elder brother Ian, better known as the creator of James Bond, served with the Naval Intelligence Division and was a close friend of Dennis Wheatley. Fleming was also a friend of Evelyn Waugh, and may have been reminded of the myth by the publication of Men at Arms in 1952. In his otherwise excellent book, Fleming devoted a considerable amount of space to debunking the mid-September mystery of bodies burned and washed ashore. Regrettably, Fleming contrived to get his facts wrong at almost every turn, and since his flawed account has been relied upon by a number of subsequent historians, it merits close analysis here. In Fleming's opinion:

In one strange case credulity found itself allied not with fear but with hope. At the beginning of September a rumour spread swiftly through the country that large numbers of dead German soldiers had been washed up on the south coast. In many accounts the corpses were said to be burnt or charred, and it was widely believed that the RAF had somehow 'set the sea on fire' at the very moment when an invasion was being launched. 'The Channel is white with dead' was a phrase in common use to describe a grim but satisfactory spectacle.

Although watchers on the south coast could see for themselves that the statement was quite untrue as far as their own sector was concerned, the rumour ran as strongly there as in other parts of the country. No corpses had come ashore here, the enquirer would be told at A; but further along the coast at B the Sappers had been called in to clear the harbour. From B he would be re-directed to C, where (it was said) a large part of the civilian population had been evacuated because of the stench.

Digging deeper, Fleming observed that:

Here again, as so often in this period, we find the flinty soil of fact bearing a crop of legend. Not only was it believed in Britain that the countless German corpses washed up in the south coast had suffered burning in the sea, but on the other side of the Channel rumours of deaths or injuries to German troops from this cause were current. An American correspondent [Shirer] in Germany saw a hospital train all of whose occupants were said to be suffering from burns, and a story circulated in various forms that the Germans had been testing flame-proof asbestos suits with disastrous results. It is inconceivable that tests of untried equipment of this type would have been carried out on a large scale or caused a noticeable number of casualties, and the origins of this particular legend remain inscrutable.

All of which was broadly accurate. Thereafter, however, Fleming allowed scepticism to cloud his judgement:

A characteristic (and from a psychoanalytical standpoint perhaps a significant) feature of the rumour was that the corpses were always supposed to have arrived not on deserted stretches of the coast, but in harbours, on municipal seafronts, and at other places where they were a public nuisance.

This was untrue, as the arrival of Poncke's body at Littlestone clearly demonstrates. Indeed had Fleming troubled to research the available material more thoroughly he might have avoided the catalogue of errors which followed. For although he hints at having investigated the riddle at some length, Fleming was apparently unaware of texts such as Blue Pencil Admiral or The Big Lie, or the Times report on October 22nd 1940, or even of Attlee's reply to the Commons in November 1946.

Instead Fleming settled on Churchill's account, inferring 'with respect' that the British war leader had succumbed to believing his own propaganda:

In fact the whole business was much odder than would appear from Churchill's narrative, for his first sentence - which gives the rumour some foundation in fact - has no such foundation itself. The recovery from the sea of 40 dead German soldiers would have had at least four consequences which would still be traceable today. It would have been reported in the war diaries of the Army formations in whose sectors they were washed up; the casualties would have been notified to the German Government through the International Red Cross in the same way as casualties to aircrews or prisoners of war in British territory; the pay books and other personal documents of the dead men would have been studied and commented on by MI14; and particulars of the West Country churchyards or cemeteries where the bodies were buried would have been recorded by the Imperial War Graves Commission. None of these consequences ensued.

Quite how far Fleming could have explored these avenues is open to question. In 1957 both MI14 files and regional War Diaries remained firmly closed, even to men of trust such as Fleming. Moreover Red Cross records remain rigorously confidential in all territories, while the records held by the Imperial War Graves Commission and Deutsche Dienstelle in Britain and Germany respectively do not specify the service to which casualties belonged. The Yarmouth confusion engendered by Churchill also muddled Fleming's geography:

To reach the coast 'between the Isle of Wight and Cornwall' the 40 corpses, assuming that they started from the nearest German embarkation area (Le Havre), would have to drift a minimum distance of over 100 miles in a north-westerly direction; and they must, with respect, be written off as not less imaginary than their countless fellow-victims who were said to be whitening the whole Channel.

Again, the lonely corpse of Heinrich Poncke proves Fleming quite wrong. Fleming seems to have arrived at his conclusion before beginning his research,

William Robinson (left) and Peter Fleming (right) discuss the bodies on the beach between Hythe and St Mary's on the BBC television programme The Finest Hour in 1957. (BBC)

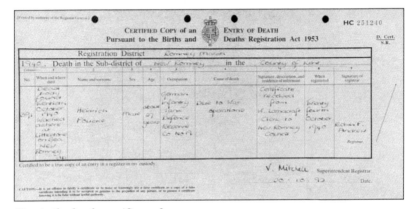

Facsimile death certificate for Heinrich Poncke, an anti-tank gunner washed ashore at Littlestone on October 20th 1940.

The jacket design for Sea Wrack, a little-known novel by Raymond Hitchcock published in 1980, which took as it's background the enigma of the bodies on the beach. (Constable)

and viewed what little evidence he chose to examine accordingly. In proving his case by recourse to unseen, unobtainable evidence, he stifled serious enquiry into the subject for more than three decades, although in fairness Fleming's errors appear to have been the result of nothing more sinister than poor scholarship and a certain haughty arrogance.

Indeed Fleming's central conclusion was correct: no large numbers of charred German soldiers were washed ashore in Britain during the summer and autumn of 1940. The debate still served to spur fresh interest in the mid-September mystery, and flushed out startling fresh evidence. In November 1957 the BBC devoted an entire edition of the television programme First Hand to the invasion summer of 1940. After advertisements were placed in coastal newspapers on both sides of the Channel, hundreds of people offered reminiscences and information. According to the Daily Mail, however, only one of the respondents shed new light on the mystery, former Royal Artillery gunner William Robinson, who recalled that:

I helped to collect the bodies of Germans from the beach between Hythe and Hastings. I was among a party of soldiers sent to search for bodies. The first day we found two soldiers. They had no badges. Later we found five more.

The programme itself, titled The Finest Hour, contained footage of PWD demonstrations staged at Moody Down Farm and Studland Bay, followed by interviews with Robinson and Peter Fleming. After running through brief details of the failed invasion, and recounting the legend that thousands of charred bodies had littered the Channel, presenter Peter West continued:

But 1553826 Gunner Robinson, 333 Battery, coastal artillery, was actually detailed to the collect the bodies from the beaches in late September.

ROBINSON: I was stationed at Herne Bay at the time, and one day I was called into the office and sent to Folkstone. I reported to Folkstone and the following day I was sent out with a party - another six or seven men - to St Mary's, also in Kent, and told to walk along the beach and collect bodies. My part of the beach was back towards Hythe. During the course of that day we found two bodies. We took the back in the lorry to a field at the back of New Romney. We left them there at a canvas screen arrangement, and there went on... and during the course of the next few days we had seven or eight more.
WEST: Were the bodies badly burned?
ROBINSON: No, slightly. On the lower part of their bodies.
WEST: How were you sure that they were German bodies?

ROBINSON: By the field-grey uniform.

WEST: Did you think that they'd been in the water very long?

ROBINSON: Yes, a considerable time.

WEST: What about identity discs, paybooks and that kind of thing?

ROBINSON: They were collected by the NCO and handed in to one of the officers at the camouflaged screen.

WEST: Do you think they might not have been pilots or aircrew of the Luftwaffe?

ROBINSON: Well, I'd seen a considerable amount of pilots both dead and alive of the Luftwaffe at the time.

WEST: What do you think yourself had happened to these Germans?

ROBINSON: Well I was told - and I believe - that they were caught by the RAF on a pre-invasion manoeuvre.

WEST: Purely on manoeuvres?

ROBINSON: Yes.

WEST: Now, I believe you were given a special sort of inducement for a rather grisly assignment.

ROBINSON: Yes - 20 Woodbines, which we collected each day, and two shillings a day, which we collected some considerable time later.

WEST: Peter Fleming is specially interested in Mr Robinson's evidence because when he was doing the research for his book Invasion 1940 he could get no official confirmation of it whatsoever.

FLEMING: Well, I am very interested. Gunner Robinson is the first man I have ever come across with first-hand experience of this particular fatigue - collecting dead Germans - and I gather that you've had evidence in the last couple of days from three or four other people all pointing to the same date at the end of September or early October. Well, there are two interesting points. One is that Sir Winston in his great book refers to this legend which we've been talking about, and specifically says that at the end of August about 40 German bodies were washed up. And it's fairly clear that the rumour which swept the country started in late August/early September started before any bodies arrived at all.

Fleming then repeated his position on unit war diaries, Red Cross notification, the Imperial War Graves Commission and intelligence reports.

WEST: So the whole thing remains a very fishy business.

FLEMING: No, I wouldn't say that, but it's still surrounded by the mystery in which it started.

WEST: Well anyway, the legend helped to keep up morale here at home.

Robinson's appearance on The Finest Hour provoked no little debate in the vicinity of Romney Marsh. According to a diarist in the Folkstone and Hythe Gazette:

I hope you didn't miss Friday night's excellent BBC television programme The Finest Hour... It was of special local interest. More than that, it again focused the spotlight on those reports about burned bodies of Germans, preparing for the invasion on the other side of the Channel, being washed ashore on the south coast.

One of those taking part in the programme, Mr WL Robinson, now a jobbing gardener in Brighton, said he was serving in the Royal Artillery in 1940 when he was sent to Folkestone and then on to St Mary's Bay to keep a watch for German bodies. One day, Mr Robinson said, two bodies were found and then later seven or eight more. As far as he knew they were buried in a mass grave at New Romney.

The mystery of those bodies, however, remains, for Chief Inspector LA Hadlow, Kent County Constabulary, who was in charge of the Hythe Sub-Division throughout the war, only recalls the finding of one body, and that was in November 1940, at Littlestone.

On Friday, a few hours before the programme was timed to go out, Miss Nancy Thomas, one of the producers, told me they had received a message from a man in Bristol informing them that during this critical period he had served in the 7th Battalion Somerset Light Infantry at Littlestone with Cyril Goodburn, of the Village Hall, Cheriton High Street.

Wondering whether ex-Private Goodburn could throw any light on the mystery of the bodies I traced him to his home at 16 Hawkins Road, Cheriton, during the weekend. He served with his battalion first at Dymchurch and then at Littlestone, from the last week in June to the following November, but he knew nothing of any German bodies being washed up although they maintained constant patrols from Littlestone to almost Dungeness.

On September 3rd men of the Somerset Light Infantry had been instrumental in apprehending Charles van den Kieboom and Sjoerd Pons, two ill-prepared German spies who arrived by boat near Dymchurch. Neither Hadlow and

83

Goodburn refute Robinson's evidence. Hadlow refers to a single body at Littlestone in November, but obviously refers to Heinrich Ponke, whose arrival on October 20th coincided with a second Luftwaffe corpse in the same area. That Goodburn knew of no bodies at all (despite Poncke's arrival) raises more questions that it answers. Furthermore, patrols between Littlestone and Dungeness have little bearing on bodies said to have been located between St Mary's and Hythe, several miles to the north.

All things considered, there seems no reason to doubt the truth of William Robinson's testimony. If true, the secrecy surrounding the disposal of the bodies near New Romney begs many questions. However, official silence, and the false orthodoxy that not one German soldier had been washed ashore in 1940, served to sow the seeds of a yet another mystery, which bloomed on the Suffolk coast at Shingle Street in 1992.

SHINGLE STREET - SMOKE WITHOUT FIRE

The isolated fishing hamlet of Shingle Street lies on a wild and desolate stretch of the Suffolk coast, twelve miles east of Ipswich. Many maps omit the village, perhaps justifiably, for visitors will find there few amenities. Its public house, the Lifeboat Inn, was blasted by scientists from the Chemical Defence Research Establishment in 1943, while many of the surviving properties are now fairweather holiday homes.

Yet this apparently unremarkable village is surrounded by mystery. To the north lies Orfordness. A secret site since the First World War, the island has played host to a bewildering variety of hush-hush military installations, including an RAF experimental flying field, and, in 1935, the first Air Ministry radar station. Postwar residents included the Atomic Weapons Research Establishment. In 1993 Orfordness, by then half wilderness, half military junkyard, was sold by the Ministry of Defence to the National Trust for £292,500. A few miles to the south, on the mouth of River Deben, stands Bawdsey Manor. This striking neo-Jacobean mansion succeeded Orfordness as the principal Air Ministry radar research establishment in 1936, and following the outbreak of war served as a regular Chain Home radar station. During the 1960's three of the four 360-foot steel masts were demolished to make way for a Bloodhound missile site. After decommissioning, RAF Bawdsey was sold for use as a language school in 1994, the final TX mast being demolished in 2000 amidst some controversy.

Sandwiched between Bawdsey and Orfordness, at the centre of Hollesley Bay, Shingle Street also boasts a secret history. At the Public Record Office lies a slim, yellowing Ministry of Home Security dossier detailing 'Evacuation of civil population from the village of Shingle Street in East Suffolk.' Indexed as HO 207/1175, its contents were to have remained secret until 2021. When first located on index in 1974, the existence of this sealed file boggled minds across East Anglia. It was all to do with a secret bomb, some hinted, while others found room for the Ultra secret. Then, in 1992, allegations that a German raiding force had been burned to death at Shingle Street in 1940 exploded across the national press. The rumours soon multiplied to include fatal chemical warfare trials, and a suppressed friendly-fire disaster in 1944. The result was the kind of undignified media scramble triggered by the Hitler Diaries, involving public outcry, the tabling of questions in the House of Commons, robust denials of a conspiracy by the Ministry of Defence, and the early declassification of file HO 207/1175.

In truth, the reality of Shingle Street's wartime past was more prosaic. Prior to the outbreak of the Second World War, Shingle Street had subsisted as a prosperous fishing hamlet for two centuries. The village boasted a prodigious smuggling history, which revolved around Dumb-Boy Cottage on the Hollesley road. Indeed in 1860 the Reverend Richard Cobbold chose Shingle Street as the setting for the climactic scene of his historical melodrama The History of Margaret Catchpole, in which the smuggler Will Laud is shot down by Revenue agents while escaping to sea. Seventy-four years later, in 1934, the village also featured prominently in Dennis Wheatley's adventure thriller Black August, set against the background of a communist coup after which Shingle Street is turned into a improvised fortress. By 1939 the village still consisted of just 23 dwellings, the most substantial of which was a line of stoutly-built coastguard cottages. The Mission Hall, at which gatherings were held once a month, was tended by a visiting parson from Alderton. There were no cars, and even the humble bicycle was an uncommon sight. The only pub, the Lifeboat Inn, had been built by Francis Langmaid on the proceeds of salvage money gained from the operation of a lifeboat prior to the foundation of the RNLI.

The outbreak of war initially affected only the coastguard personnel. Although part of the station had been sold off, the observation building was retained for use by the four local men who continued to act as Auxiliaries: Eric Andrews, Ronald Harris, Bert Simpson and Will Lucock. Their duties included patrolling the beach as far as Bawdsey East Lane each evening, a return distance of about four miles, with their counterparts from Bawdsey responsible for the morning patrol. This wearying routine proved short-lived, for in November 1939 the 2/4th Battalion The Essex Regiment arrived to defend a lengthy stretch of the East Suffolk coastline. A Territorial unit, battalion headquarters were located at Saxmundham, with forward companies deployed at Leiston and Aldeburgh. The regimental history recalls:

That curious period of lull and unreality which occurred after the outbreak of war, with little to enliven the long hours of guard duty and training. There was the occasional mine on the shore, flares and gunfire well out to sea as some east coast convoy was attacked, and the sound of aircraft engines by night as enemy aeroplanes flew in to drop magnetic mines in harbours or on the coastal sea routes. There was also an occasional spy scare to break monotony and keep sentries on their toes.

One such scare was the theft of a petty cash box from the office of Lieutenant Colonel Lord Edward Hay, the Battalion Commander, under cover of the Christmas festivities at Sizewell Hall. Since the cash box allegedly contained

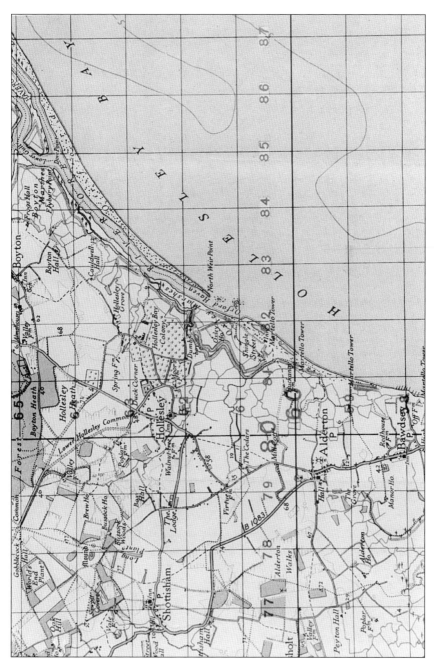

OS map of Shingle Street and surrounding area printed by the War Office in 1941, issued to the coastguard station. (Michael Lucock)

plans of local defences and minefields, its loss lead to several NCOs from the guard detail being reduced to the ranks.

One local historian, the late Derek Johnson, has claimed that one bleak winter night an entire patrol from the 2/4th Essex vanished without trace from the shore at Shingle Street. According to his source, never precisely revealed, each night wireless-equipped patrols numbering half a dozen men were dispatched to watch over particularly isolated beaches. The story runs that a patrol covering Shingle Street inexplicably ceased to report, and were placed on a charge in their absence. The next morning a search party discovered scattered equipment on the beach, but no trace of the lost patrol.

Since no official records confirm the story it remains at best apocryphal. Tom Abram, an infantry soldier stationed by the beach at Bawdsey during the summer of 1940, puts the tale in perspective:

I never heard of any patrols equipped with wireless sets, although rumours of shore patrols missing from their positions were commonplace. We heard the same thing when we were stationed at Norman's Bay, near Bexhill-on-Sea.

In April 1940 the 2/4th Essex moved to Northumberland, and were replaced until November by the Liverpool Scottish. Meanwhile June 1940 saw the fall of France, and the creation of a coastal Defence Area roughly 20 miles in depth between Southend-on-Sea and King's Lynn. In July the evacuation zone was extended south as far as Portland in Dorset. In East Anglia alone, no less than 127,000 people were obliged to leave coastal towns to make way for an extensive network of fixed defences, minefields included. In line with this policy the Regional Commissioner for the Eastern Region, Will Spens, ordered the complete evacuation of Shingle Street on June 22nd 1940. Issued under Regulation 16(a) of the Defence (General) Regulations 1939, the order was to take effect before midnight on the 25th, leaving villagers just three days to find alternative accommodation. Only the coastguard personnel were exempt.

This measure, while draconian, was highly prudent. Work had already begun on an extensive minefield running east from Oxley Farm towards the beach, then south along the shore ridge to Bawdsey East Lane. The danger posed by these primitive devices was underlined by the death of one hapless Royal Engineer charged with laying them. Worse, the one road leading out of the village towards Hollesley crossed a narrow humpbacked bridge at Dumb-Boy Sluice. This too had been mined, and at Action Stations was to be blown without further orders. Since several natural watercourses had also been widened to create an anti-tank ditch, the hamlet and its inhabitants would have been rapidly - and hopelessly - cut off in the event of a genuine emergency.

Although very necessary, the evacuation caused no little hardship. The majority of the villagers moved to Hollesley two miles away, while others chose Bawdsey and Alderton. With just one lorry to assist in the hasty exodus, villagers were able to remove only the barest essentials, and many larger chattels such as furniture had to be left behind. In a letter addressed to Spens in August one elderly widow complained:

Dear Sir,
I am writing to ask if you can help me in the evacuation of Shingle Street. Mr Hocking and Mr Collett came round and told us to take 48 hours notice to get out. The military helped me move some of my furniture. I am a widow getting ten shillings a week and lived in my own home. Now I am turned out and having to pay six shillings a week rent. Since our evacuation my house has been broken into by the soldiers, windows smashed and doors broken from hinges, and also goods taken from the house. Can you give me the paper with the orders to quit my home which I should have had at the time, or can you help me and give me advice on what steps to take?

Sadly, over the next few months extensive looting took place, although servicemen who behaved in this way formed a tiny minority. Tom Abram, a private with the Liverpool Scottish stationed at Bawdsey East Lane, recalls the humdrum routine of Home Defence units stationed on the Suffolk coast during the 'invasion summer' of 1940:

Our platoon was ordered to man certain points near and on the beach. We were billeted in tents which had been erected alongside a field near the beach road. Other platoons were stationed near Shingle Street. We were close to the Martello Tower, which was manned by the coastguard. There was also a cottage in which lived two sisters who provided much needed tea and cakes.

We hadn't been there long when the Royal Engineers turned up with very unsophisticated anti-tank mines, which were laid in the field alongside our tents, with our help and a little instruction. They then mined the beach, although with the movement of the shingle it became a very dangerous place. I often wonder if all the mines were ever lifted. Tales were told that the Sappers suffered casualties. There was a profound lack of action. Whenever enemy fighter planes passed over on their way to Martlesham Heath we had a go with our Bren gun, but with only one

The rear of the Lifeboat Inn, early 1943. (CDRE)

Shingle Street in 1928, viewed from the Martello Tower looking north. (Michael Lucock)

The Lifeboat Inn, circa 1920s. (Michael Lucock)

Shingle Street, March 1943. A group of RAF and Porton Down personnel mark the occasion of the CDRE mustard bomb test, together with local police and firemen. Percy Darvell (second right) stated in 1992 that the civilian scientist in the centre was Barnes Wallis, but doubt has been cast on this claim. (Percy Darvell)

Two further pre-war views of Shingle Street (Michael Lucock)

tracer bullet to every ten rounds it was futile. In June and later on we had Stand To from sunset to dawn with orders to hold on at all costs. It must be remembered that in those days we had no wireless, never saw a newspaper, never received information from our superiors, and never saw any road signs or maps. We simply lived from day to day and did as we were told.

Although there were constant warnings about imminent invasion the only German we saw was a dead airman who we fished out of the sea and carried back to camp on a hurdle.

The German flyer, washed ashore at Bawdsey on October 30th 1940, almost certainly belonged to the same crew as a second man found near Hollesley that same day, as well as a third at Shingle Street on the 29th. A fourth man had been washed ashore two days previously at Aldeburgh. All had been in the water for nearly a month, their Heinkel 111 having come down off the Suffolk coast on October 4th. This sad quartet, the only Germans officially acknowledged as having landed near Shingle Street during the Second World War, scarcely posed any great military threat.

Ronald Harris, an Auxiliary Coastguard at Shingle Street throughout the war, recalls that on one occasion written instructions were received from the area coastguard headquarters at Walton-on-the-Naze to watch the shoreline for charred bodies. Mr Harris does not recall the date, and in any case saw none. Indeed the only enemy landing in Hollesley Bay took the form of a theoretical 11 Corps exercise on July 29th, which unfolded thus:

14.50 Enemy troops landing in Dovercourt Bay... 15.10 Confused fighting in Woodbridge... 15.22 Frinton and Mersea captured... 15.23 Ipswich heavily damaged and many casualties. Strong enemy force arrived on outskirts of town from Harwich... 15.47 Sniped en-route at Ashbocking and Otley... 16.00 Enemy landing one mile south of Shingle Street...

Sadly, the outcome of this close-run paper battle is not recorded. On September 25th, however, an equally interesting entry was made in the War Diary of the 165th Infantry Brigade, covering Hollesley Bay:

Received a letter from [55] Division stating that a scheme was afoot to produce an impenetrable barrage of flame on the sea to prevent or destroy enemy ships attempting a landing.

The following day the unit dispatched its reply, indicating that flame barrages were required off the following localities:

a) Bawdsey 8057
b) Mouth of River Deben 7855
c) Mouth of River Orwell 7249
d) Felixstowe, from Ferry 7755 to Landguard Fort 7350

The history of the sea flame barrage research programme, and of the PWD, was related in detail in Chapter Two. Available records show that of the few operational barrages installed, one was a small stretch at Wick in Scotland, and another an experimental length at Shoeburyness, with a crude anti-seaplane device also tested near Wroxham on the Norfolk Broads. Beyond these sites, there is no evidence that any other flame barrages were constructed on the east coast of Britain, or that the 165th Brigade's war diary represents anything more than a routine, and premature, recommendation.

In October 1941, with the threat of invasion having faded, the War Office wrote to the Ministry of Home Security to indicate that Shingle Street might now be de-requisitioned. However, it was decided that civilians would not be allowed to return to their homes due to the continued danger posed by beach mines, which had by now accounted for another two soldiers and a trespassing civilian. Then, in September 1942, events took an more sinister turn.

At this time the Chemical Defence Research Establishment at Porton Down were casting around for an area of land, replete with buildings, on which to conduct trials with a new chemical weapon. On their behalf the Ministry of Home Security approached the twelve Regional Commissioners, to request:

Suitable evacuated dwelling houses in reasonably good repair, which [the CDRE] could use for the purpose of dropping trials of 250-lb HE/Chem bombs. The height of release of the bombs would be between 500 ft and 1000 ft. The bomb wall thickness would be 1/4 inch, and its content would be 75 lbs TNT, together with a charging of either mustard or a substitute.

The Ministry went on to indicate that existing battle training areas were preferable, since in these areas considerable damage had already been inflicted on buildings and property. Following assurances that the inmates of the nearby Hollesley Bay borstal would not be effected by blast or poison gas, the CDRE were granted leave to bomb Shingle Street. The trials were expected to last between seven and ten days, and would involve pinpoint low level bombing. In turn, Porton Down was informed of the approximate value of all 20 properties, so that the question of compensation could be taken up with the Ministry of Home Security at a later date.

Weather conditions meant that the trial was delayed for several months. A measure of the perceived importance of the device tested was supplied in 1974 by the late Nora Pierce Butler, a native of Woodbridge. In 1943 Miss Pierce Butler met Air Commodore Patrick Huskinson, the blinded Director of Armament Development at the Air Ministry. Their meeting was in a social context, but on learning that Miss Butler knew Shingle Street well, Huskinson told her in confidence that a new type of bomb would shortly be tested on the village. 'There won't be any Shingle Street next week,' he warned ominously.

The trial itself, delayed until March 28th 1943, was witnessed by several civilians interviewed for this book. Following the evacuation of the coastguards, large yellow target markers were painted around the Lifeboat Inn. Percy Darvell, then an Auxiliary Fireman, recalls that his crew were called out from Woodbridge for several dry runs before a twin-engined aircraft flew in low from the south and released the bomb, scoring a direct hit on the Lifeboat Inn. The blast damage to the pub and the surrounding cottages was both extensive and precise, causing the scientist overseeing the trial to rub his hands gleefully. In 1992 Darvell claimed that the boffin concerned was none other than Barnes Wallis, the legendary aircraft and bomb designer, whose creations included the device deployed by 617 Squadron against the Ruhr dams in May 1943. However, Wallis was not involved in any Porton Down research, while his diary records no visits to Suffolk during 1943, and the civilian in the photograph provided by Darvell is not recognised as Wallis by his family.

In 1994 Porton Down revealed that the device dropped at Shingle Street was an experimental 250 lb high explosive/chemical bomb, designed to enhance the tactical use of mustard gas by use of a bomb containing both a vesicant charge and high explosive, thus combining both damage and contamination, and dispensing with the need to co-ordinate a mixed stick of separate chemical and explosive weapons. The bomb contained four gallons of dyed methyl salicylate, otherwise known as oil of wintergreen, an innocuous mustard substitute which could be readily traced by sight and smell in order to show the extent of the chemical contamination. Ultimately the test was judged a failure, as the instantaneous fusing necessary to prevent the chemical charge being buried in the ground in turn diminished the effectiveness of the high explosive.

Damage of another kind was inflicted after the arrival of the US 8th Air Force in East Anglia. In the scramble to build new airfields across the region, thousands of tons of shingle was systematically removed from the beach to provide hard core for runways. This was achieved at some cost to the environment, since the sea has crept roughly 40 yards closer to the houses since extraction ceased in 1944.

In addition to the CDRE mustard bomb, spring 1943 saw other secret weapons arrive in the area. To the north of Shingle Street and Hollesley lay the Orford Battle Training Area, whose residents included the 79th Armoured Division. In April 1943 the 79th had been reorganised as an armoured engineering unit equipped with 'Funnies' - specially adapted tanks designed to breach the Atlantic Wall during the D-Day landings. The Division remained in the Orford area until early 1944 and carried out much training there, pitting their vehicles against replicas of the obstacles which would be encountered on the beaches of Normandy. On at least one occasion waterproofing trials with Duplex Drive tanks were conducted at Shingle Street, although there is no evidence of any fatal accidents.

The approach of peace in Europe brought no relief for the long-suffering population. Although in October 1944 it was noted that Shingle Street had been prioritised for mine clearance before the end of the year, by April 1945 the military could only inform the Ministry of Home Security that the village remained uninhabitable, being an 'extremely dangerous and awkward minefield.' This dour assessment was all too accurate. Those houses not damaged by the 1943 bombing had suffered equally from five years of weather and neglect. Rendered uninhabitable, many were written off as total losses. A 1945 report by the Regional Commissioner on the state of all properties in the village makes for pathetic reading:

A small bungalow of brick and slate construction owned by Mrs S Curtis. Damaged by bombing beyond repair. Walls fractured, doors and window frames blown in and slates off. Evidence of some chattels which had obviously been looted. Still contains three chairs, one bed, an old settee and useless personal effects.

Bungalow of wooden construction with pan-tiled roof, owned by Mr R Harris. All windows smashed and end demolished by bombing. Total loss.

The Lifeboat Inn, of wood and lathe and plaster construction with pan-tiled roof. Completely demolished.

The partial devastation wrought on the Lifeboat Inn by the CDRE had been largely completed two years later by a raiding party from Bawdsey Manor, who dynamited the shell of the Inn for its timber while constructing a VE Day bonfire.

The removal of the beach mines lasted well into 1945, and residents who wished to return to the blasted village were obliged to wait years, rather than months. The compensation offered was meagre, and much delayed due to Whitehall wrangling between the War Office and the Ministry of Home Security. Ronald Harris, whose bungalow Ronina beside the Lifeboat Inn had been damaged beyond repair, would wait until 1949 for a new, more permanent house to be completed. Even as late as 1948, Archie White described the once 'busy and prosperous' hamlet as 'blown to pieces' with nothing left but 'large deep ponds between the houses and the sea to show where the river once ran.'

Plans to build a new Lifeboat Inn were thwarted when a Mrs Pritchard-Carr won the single available victualler's licence and opened a tea shop. Shingle Street never regained its status as a working fishing village, and instead became the near-exclusive domain of the weekend fisherman, the watercolour artist and the hardy rambler.

And then, in 1992, the ill-briefed journalist hungry for a scoop on the invasion that failed.

On March 7th 1992 the tranquil postwar slumber of Hollesley Bay was disturbed by an arresting article published in the East Anglian Daily Times. Beneath the headline DOZENS OF SOLDIERS KILLED IN NAZI INVASION BLUNDER, journalist Henry Creagh revealed to readers that:

Dozens of British soldiers were burnt to death by one of their own men in a wartime exercise on the Suffolk coast which went tragically wrong, it was claimed yesterday. New information has come to the EADT about the secret of Shingle Street, an isolated coastal hamlet which was evacuated in 1940 for use by the armed forces. The incident allegedly occurred during a training exercise near the radar installation at Bawdsey, just south of Shingle Street.

Part of the base's defences consisted of drums of petrol chained to concrete blocks under the sea and wired to detonators. In case of an enemy assault from the sea, the drums would be blown and the petrol would rise to the surface, where it could be set alight using tracer rounds.

The Army had decided to carry out a mock assault on Bawdsey, and contacted the base to say it would be doing so, but somehow the message was not passed on. Later that night, a sentry saw rubber dinghies approaching the base, and, assuming it was the enemy, detonated the charges. The petrol was set alight by tracer bullets from a machine gun post. Many soldiers died in the inferno and their bodies were carried out on the tide, only to be washed up at Shingle Street.

Mr Ron Harris, one of the few residents to remain in Shingle Street after the evacuation, was a coastguard at the site throughout the war. He can remember being given an order to look for charred bodies, but cannot recall the date or any incident where the sea was set on fire.

A file on the mystery has lain in the Public Records Office since the Second World War under a 75-year embargo lasting until 2014. Such an embargo can only be granted for reasons of national security, to protect confidential information supplied by the public, or where publication of records would distress or embarrass any living person. The Ministry of Defence could not comment on the claims.

The EADT source was said to be an anonymous telephone caller 'close to the Ministry of Defence', who had seen the classified papers by chance. Although the MoD mole allegedly telephoned on a second occasion, the EADT news desk were given no name or contact number, and the source fell silent after the story broke nationally in wildly exaggerated form. Crucially, Creagh's report omitted one important detail: the tragedy was said to have occurred during training for the Normandy landings, presumably in 1944. The phrases 'Nazi invasion blunder' and '1940' painted an altogether more colourful picture, as subsequent developments would prove.

In truth, the Shingle Street mystery was already old news, the EADT having published broadly similar allegations on two previous occasions. On August 3rd 1974, in an article titled WAR FILE ON HAMLET CLOSED FOR 40 YEARS, the existence of HO 207/1175 was revealed to the public for the first time:

The contents of the war government's file on the tiny Suffolk coast hamlet of Shingle Street are to remain secret for another 40 years. Other secrets, like those of the War Cabinet, were de-classified and released to the Public Records Office in London after 30 years. But the file indexed 'Evacuation of civil population from the village of Shingle Street, East Suffolk' has been given a 75-year embargo.

Officials responsible for the government archives say that embargoes of this duration are generally imposed on papers believed to contain matters of 'personal sensitivity' likely to cause embarrassment or even distress to members of the public. Records remained closed on two other general grounds - because they contained matters affecting state security or information given to government departments under a pledge of confidentiality. They did not know which category the Shingle Street file came under. The maximum embargo is 100 years.

Mr Norman Scarfe, the Suffolk historian, who lives in Shingle Street, said yesterday he could not imagine what might be in the file that made it so confidential. 'What happened was that everyone had to move out when the Army took the place over as a battle training area. There was only a very small population and most of them went to Hollesley, only a mile or two away. When the war was over they came back here. I have never heard anyone grousing about what happened. Some of the houses were badly knocked about because in some mysterious way they were used as a target for bombing, I believe.'

Digging deeper into the mystery, reporter Margaret Warren caught the Ministry of Defence in unusually playful mood, an enigmatic spokesman hinting that:

This has been classified as Top Secret, and as we are not going to release it for another 45 years you might say that it is Top Top Secret. This embargo usually only applies when it comes to something of national importance.

Phrases as loaded as 'Top Top Secret' and 'national security' tickled fancies across East Anglia. Yet nowhere, either in 1974 or at any subsequent time, was it reported that the 75 year embargo placed on HO207/1175 was in no way unique, for in fact all files relating to the wartime requisition of land and property by the military also remained sealed. That innocuous dossiers on the 'Immobilisation of boats (1939-1941)' and 'Agricultural damage: Thetford battle training area' also remained closed should have hinted that the yellowing pages contained little affecting national security. Moreover Ministry of Home Security files are largely concerned with the civilian population, and only indirectly with military matters. Almost by definition, therefore, any account of a disastrous Allied exercise near the Bawdsey radar station, let alone a bungled raid by German commandos, lay well beyond the ambit of HO207/1175.

In 1984 another EADT journalist, David Henshall, indulged in further speculation when details of Exercise Tiger first reached a wider public. The facts behind the Slapton Sands disaster, in which 749 Americans died after German E-boats intercepted a large-scale D-Day rehearsal off Dorset in April 1944, were less secret than obscure. Undaunted, beneath the headline D-DAY: SUFFOLK'S OWN SINISTER SECRET, the EADT speculated on:

Another D-Day exercise in which British barges were blown out of the water by British gunners who had not been told what was going on... Defenders set fire to the sea in the belief that the enemy was about to land on British soil. The soldiers were said to number about 100, dying when trapped by a new invention codenamed PLUTO.

Henshall was vague as to his sources, and thereafter the Normandy slant on the Shingle Street myth remained dormant. Four years later, in 1978, local historian Derek Johnson published a rather fanciful theory about atomic missile tests in his book East Anglia at War. Subsequently, in June 1989, at a time when he was not engaged in active research on the subject, Johnson claims to have received a mysterious telephone call from a 'Mr Smith', sternly warning him off further investigation of all wartime events at Shingle Street. To their eternal regret, no other investigator has received such a call. Then, in March 1992, the EADT report of a 'NAZI INVASION BLUNDER' added substance to the 'D-DAY SINISTER SECRET' hinted at eight years earlier. As a result of a friendly-fire incident, it was alleged, dozens of Allied soldiers had burned to death in Hollesley Bay. Had the potential of the rumour as a news story - and as history - ended there, coverage of this cyclical tale might well have died away for another decade. But instead it got stranger.

On the strength of the EADT report on March 7th, Long Melford gallery owner John Rux Burton came forward with information passed on my his late grandfather, John Edgar Burton. The facts as stated to this author ran as follows. When war broke out in 1939 John Edgar Burton abandoned his London accountancy practice to scour the countryside for wood. This innocuous task served as cover for oblique intelligence duties, Edgar Burton apparently reporting to the Naval Intelligence Division. According to his grandson, one day during the autumn of 1940:

He was told that a German force had attempted to invade Suffolk and was dispatched to Shingle Street to find out what had happened. When he arrived the beach was covered with dozens upon dozens of bodies, most of them charred beyond recognition. The defenders believed the men to Germans dressed as British soldiers. A senior officer then arrived on the scene and said that the bodies were really those of British troops, and that there had been a friendly-fire incident. My grandfather was not convinced, since the markings on a burned-out dinghy nearby appeared to be German. The dinghy was then heaved onto the back of a truck and driven away, along with the bodies. He thought that the government were very keen on not allowing it out that these men had died by burning in oil in the sea.

Although he continued to work as an intelligence officer, Edgar Burton heard nothing more of the incident. He came to discuss it with his family only later in life, when memories of the horrific scene began to provoke nightmares.

Forgotten by historians since Peter Fleming in the late 1950s, the re-emergence of the myth of the invasion that failed in 1992 set the media hares running. First on the scene was the Sunday Telegraph, whose defence correspondent Christy Campbell pondered across a double-page spread: 'Wartime rumours of a failed Nazi invasion have resurfaced. Was there a cover-up, or is the story just too good to be left alone?' The answer concocted by stampeding hacks succeeded in covering both bases. Treating the persuasively sensationalist Telegraph article as gospel, the media descended upon Suffolk to disinter evidence of the forgotten dead. Over the next three months a lack of thorough research, combined with an overweening desire to produce eyecatching copy, saw the publication of a kaleidoscopic catalogue of errors and half-truths. Worse, the confused reportage was based largely upon letters and calls from members of the public, with the result that confused juxtaposition of the 1940 invasion myth, the 1943 CDRE bombing, and the alleged 1944 training disaster served only to cloud already muddied waters.

Between March and July 1992 a comprehensive overview of coverage of the Shingle Street mystery reveals a bewildering array of misplaced and unreliable theories. Besides endless variations of the mid-September mystery of failed invasion, it was claimed that: civilians spent two days clearing bodies from the shoreline at Felixstowe; ditto at Great Yarmouth; a skeleton found by a party from the Hollesley borstal in June 1985 was that of a Nazi; Germans landed in Suffolk on motorbikes and lobbed grenades at coastal gun batteries; the dead men at Shingle Street in British uniforms were German Brandenburg commandos; the RAF had bombed civilians; German POW's were used as guinea pigs in a chemical warfare trial; experiments with amphibious tanks by the 79th Armoured Division led to tragedy. Author Jack Higgins was pressed for a quote, observing that the 'really astonishing' thing was how fiction and reality can blur. An investigative nadir was reached when Konrad Burg's dubious account of an east coast foray by the Waffen SS was reproduced beneath a variety of creative headlines, such as INVASION MET FIRE WALL and NAZI LANDING ATTEMPT DISASTER REPORT FOUND. Fortunately, no mention was made of Dennis Wheatley's 1934 novel Black August, despite the vivid image conjured by the chapter titled Burn Them! Burn Them! One could have been forgiven for thinking that Charles Barbe, Robert Solborg and Lars Moen were back on the case.

The industrious Derek Johnson reported having discovered that staff at Ipswich Crematorium had been instructed to rush all available coffins to Shingle Street, a distance of some 20 miles. At roadblocks close the village the trucks were stopped and the cargo transferred to military vehicles, the civilian drivers being allowed no further. Subsequently, Mr Johnson also claimed to have uncovered evidence that bodies had been interred in a mass grave in nearby Rendlesham Forest. Thankfully the Sunday Sport lent its weight to the investigation, and their intrepid reporter was able to locate without effort: 'near Ipswich... the unmarked grave where 100 kraut stormtroopers lie secretly buried - on the orders of Churchill himself.' This story was in turn lampooned in Viz magazine, and the suspicion must remain that Johnson simply fabricated stories of burial pits, atomic tests and sinister telephone calls as publicity for his own books.

Others too stumbled across secret Nazi graves. Anglia Television News broadcast pictures of the graves of several unknown German servicemen from around the region. In fact, the generic inscription Eine Deutsche Soldat applies to casualties for all three services, and their presence is due to nothing more mysterious than practical difficulties over the removal of all German remains to Cannock Chase after 1959. Other mistakes were the result of misleading spin. Hollis Fowler, formerly a Home Guard in Holbrook, recalled a dark night spent scouring the countryside for suspected invaders:

We were told that the sea had been set alight, and to watch out for anyone because the Germans had landed. We had orders to stop anything and everything we saw, and not to mention a thing about it to anybody else... Not that I saw anything!

Hollis Fowler's recollection was originally printed in the EADT, which failed to mention that Mr Fowler did not arrive in Holbrook until 1943. Instead, triggered by wartime memories of the 1940 invasion myth, the story which achieved predominance was that Germany had, in the words of Anglia News: 'attempted to invade the Suffolk coast in regimental or brigade strength to establish a toehold and/or act as a decoy for a main invasion on the south coast.'

The key to the enigma, it was widely held, lay at the PRO within the pages of file HO207/1175, and with few prepared to wait until the year 2021 to examine the contents of the sealed PRO file, pressure began to mount for its early declassification. Naturally enough, the burden initially fell upon local MPs, Shingle Street itself falling within the Suffolk Coastal constituency of John Gummer, then Minister for Agriculture. In May, following media prompting, Gummer promised to raise the matter privately with the Home Secretary, Kenneth Clarke. A more effective campaign was launched by Jamie Cann, the newly-elected Labour MP for Ipswich. After writing to the Home Secretary to request that the PRO file be opened, Cann told reporters he believed that 'the people of Suffolk have a right to know what went on in their own backyard over 50 years ago.' Clarke informed Cann that the matter would be given due consideration, no doubt as part of a governmental pledge of greater 'openness' regarding official secrecy. Sealed files on the Hess affair released in June had proved innocuous, however, and Clarke's gesture served only to convince sceptics that truly sensitive material still stood little chance of passing the blue pencil of latterday censors unscathed.

Anticipation reached fever pitch on the evening of July 6th, when the Home Secretary announced that HO207/1175 would be opened to the public the following morning. The reaction of the Daily Telegraph was typical of many:

VEIL LIFTED ON WARTIME EVACUATION: The wartime mystery behind the unexplained evacuation of a Suffolk fishing hamlet will soon be solved... It was thought the dead men were German commandos sent to attack an RAF radar station at nearby Bawdsey Manor...

According to the EADT:

The wartime secret of Shingle Street will finally be revealed today after a relentless campaign by the EADT... The file will explain exactly what happened during World War Two at Shingle Street, when dozens of charred bodies in British uniforms were washed up on the beach... Whitehall has until now refused to say who the men in British uniforms were, how they died or where they came from... EADT reporters were travelling to the PRO in London this morning to view the files for the first time.

Although the sudden release of the file caught many unawares, a red-eye wire from Associated Press drew a crowd of ill-briefed tabloid reporters to the PRO. Those eager for a scoop of historical proportions were sorely disappointed. Instead of a thwarted German assault, the file merely detailed mundane wrangles over compensation for damaged property, and the minor revelation that an (uncharged) mustard gas bomb had been dropped at the village in 1943.

Six other HO207 files relating to the Eastern Region were also released. They were, if anything, even less revealing than the Shingle Street papers. HO207/1183, concerning Iken Hall near Woodbridge, revealed:

The lady has always been very reasonable in her questions with regard to military activities around her house, and in view of the use of it as a residential war nursery, I think it will be appreciated how important it is not to involve the children in risk of damage or unnecessary alarm.

One dare not ponder the consequences had this secret intelligence fallen into unscrupulous foreign hands. Indeed so damp was the squib that few national newspapers bothered to report the story the following day. Meanwhile Anglia News cried foul, voicing a suspicion that its contents had been 'raided in an official cover-up', and all reference to an attempt at invasion carefully removed by the Ministry of Defence.

Having held the front page on July 8th, the EADT was obliged to make do with a desultory resume of 'sinister theories' beneath the misleading headline SECRET FILE DEEPENS WAR TRAGEDY - HAMLET USED FOR MUSTARD GAS TESTS. An apparently genuine photograph of 'a lone angler on the beach at Shingle Street yesterday' did little to assuage local disappointment. Ipswich MP Jamie Cann was equally unhappy:

I think there has been an error made, because the Ministry of Defence have told me they are not aware of any other files relating to Shingle Street. There are so many reports about bodies being found on the beach that it must have happened, and if it happened there will be reports. And if there are reports there must be files.

This strident mood proved shortlived. A week later Cann was supplied with a superficially detailed summary of wartime events at Shingle Street prepared by the Army Historical Branch, and approved by Lord Cranborne, a junior Defence Minister. In essence, it drew from: (a) the Eastern Command War Diary for 1940; (b) a resume of wartime PWD activity; (c) the CDRE proposal and 1943 bombing trial; (d) the 79th Armoured Division war diary; (e) Attlee's written reply in November 1946; (f) Churchill's paragraph on charred bodies in Their Finest Hour. The slant offered by the Ministry was predictably sober, their overall summary concluding:

There is no evidence in either the most highly classified contemporary British records, or apparently in the contemporary German records, of an actual attempt by the Germans to land in Britain... The contemporary authoritative records provide no evidence to support the claims that a number of burnt, British uniformed bodies were washed up on the Shingle Street beach in the summer or autumn of 1940, or that the 1943 events also considered provide any evidence to support the general allegations made.

With the exception of the 1943 bombing trial, details of which had only recently surfaced through HO207/1175, none of the underwhelming material on which the Ministry apparently relied had been classified since 1974. Indeed the MoD even overlooked Blue Pencil Admiral and The Big Lie, and with hindsight the report carried little real weight. Nevertheless Cann accepted these findings, and at a press conference in Ipswich announced there had been no invasion attempt at Shingle Street, adding later:

> The truth is that not very much happened. I am convinced we now have all the information available. The only remaining mystery is why anyone wanted to cover it up for 75 years.

John Gummer also now publicly dismissed as 'nonsense' the suggestion that Nazis had attempted to wrest his constituency 50 years earlier:

> There is no reason at all to believe other than the Home Office statement. Clearly that's what did happen. I can't understand why anybody objects or disagrees.

Recognising that the puzzle was by now either solved, or unsolvable, the media withdrew. On July 20th the Daily Telegraph announced WAR RIDDLE OF BODIES ON BEACH IS SOLVED, a conclusion echoed by the Times on August 15th in a piece on the PRO and the 30 year rule. The back-peddling evidenced by the EADT was more furious still. On July 30th, hidden away on page 22, the headline SHINGLE STREET RIDDLE WAS UNRAVELLED 45 YEARS AGO presaged an article in which a correspondent dismissed all former claims as conspiracy theories. 'It's like UFOs or corn circles,' it was stated with authority. 'People want to believe it.'

Which begs the question of which came blacker - the pot, the kettle, or the propaganda? Ultimately the story of Shingle Street is the story of smoke without fire, and of two identical myths separated only by time. One, the more modern, bears witness to the boundless credulity engendered by the media age. The second, older and wiser, stands as a testament to the potent effect of unavowable black propaganda, and the desperate need of a beleaguered population eager to see light at the end of a dark tunnel.

POSTSCRIPT: LOOKED, DUCKED, VANISHED

If this text proves anything at all, it is that there was no attempt at an invasion of the British Isles in 1940, and no mass destruction of Hitler's landing fleet in mid-Channel. Rumours of small German landing parties and missing patrols were almost as common, and at first glance would seem to be just as fantastical. However, the original research conducted by this author did unearth several stories even more remarkable than those told by William Robinson, Agnes Mann, Renee Meurisse or John Edgar Burton elsewhere in this book.

Edward Sharpin, a private serving in the Royal Army Service Corps, was captured in Greece in 1941, and spent the remainder of the war in captivity in several PoW camps (18A and 18B) in Austria. It was there that he had an unexpected encounter:

I spoke German and was often used as an interpreter. In late 1943 or early 1944 I was sent down to the railway junction at Selzthal to do something or other. While there I noticed a old-looking man. He looked a dead-ringer for the actor John le Mesurier so far as I remember, with grey hair, and didn't seem very well. I went over and asked him who he was. He didn't have a pay book, and said he was in the Home Guard. He told me that he had been on guard duty on the Kent coast, and that a squad of Germans had landed and taken him away.

I think he was being paraded around different PoW camps to try to reduce the prisoners' morale. I don't think he was a plant - you could usually sense it if people were. I think he was a Londoner originally, as he mentioned something about Fulham football club.

Sharpin's remarkable escape from captivity is related in the book Greece 1941: To Fight Another Day, by William Frick. A similar man with a similar story was encountered by Jack Driscoll of the 12th Royal Lancers, at Stalag IIIVB in Upper Silesia:

I myself met this poor old man in Lamsdorf PoW camp in about 1943, while I was also in captivity. I was walking in the compound when I saw this chap with Home Guard on his shoulder. I stood back in amazement and asked if it was a joke. He told me that a party from a U-boat had landed and snatched him, while he was on duty on the Kent coast. I gather later he was repatriated via Sweden by the Red Cross.

Could this be the same man whose story was related by George Hearse to his son, also George Hearse:

From 1943 to 1945 my father worked in London in a government department. Being a 1914-18 war veteran he took part in Home Guard duties. Sometime late in 1943 there was an appeal for Home Guard personnel to volunteer for weekend guard duty in a sensitive location on the coast. One man said goodbye to his wife on the station platform in London, expecting to be home in a few days' time. His wife heard nothing more about him until several weeks later, when she was informed he was a prisoner of war in Germany. My father told me this story some time before his death in 1945, and I have no reason to doubt its authenticity.

If he ever existed, the unfortunate London Home Guard would seem not to have been an isolated case. In 1945, Mr EC Leslie was an administrative lieutenant at a transit camp at Barry in South Wales, at which returned prisoners of war were processed. When asked when and where he had been captured, one soldier in his twenties revealed to Lieutenant Leslie that he had been snatched by Germans at St Margaret's Bay in Kent in 1940. 'He seemed a bit embarrassed about it', Mr Leslie recalled in 1992.

But can these reports really have any foundation in fact? For despite the frequency with which Allied commandos and other raiding parties probed the enemy coastline between 1940 and 1944, there are no recorded incidents of German troops returning the compliment. This, of itself, seems curious, given that Germany planned to invade in 1940, and knew that an Allied invasion was coming by 1944. Yet had they done so, surely some surviving participants would have come forward to tell (or sell) their story? And with no declassified papers dropping any such historical bombshell, what possible reason could there be to leave the matter veiled in official secrecy? There is no easy answer, save that if one chooses to believe that one or two isolated sentries were snatched by small German raiding parties, their absence might have been put down to simple desertion. Obscurity, rather than secrecy, might explain why these chimerical incidents were lost to history. As for the victims, perhaps they were simply not believed on their return, just as Private Albert Pooley of the Royal Norfolk Regiment was disbelieved in 1943, after being repatriated on medical grounds and bearing news of the now-infamous massacre of 100 unarmed prisoners by SS troops at Le Paradis in May 1940. Pooley struggled for three years for his story to be accepted and investigated, even then succeeding only after corroborative evidence from France and a fellow survivor came to light.

On the snatched Home Guards, however, the final verdict must remain Not Proven.

CHAPTERS 1 and 2

Ansel ....(1960)
Banks ....(1946)
Churchill ....(1949)
Collier ....(1979)
Daily Express 26.8.44
Lampe ....(1968)
Langford.........................(1979)
McKee...........................(1960)
Medlicott - unpublished paper
Roskill...........................(1970) (1974)
Schenk...........................(1990)
SIPRI............................(1975)
West.............................(1992)
Wheatley ....(1959)
PRO documents:
AVIA 15/588
CAB 4/6
PREM 3/264
SUPP 15/2
ADM 116/4571
WO 279/203
WO 193/734
Correspondence with and interviews by author.

CHAPTER 3

Agar ....(1959)
Banks ....(1946)
Bowyer..........................(1974)
PRO documents:
PREM 3/264
WO 193/734

CHAPTER 4

Colville..........................(1985)
Roskill...........................(1954)
White............................(1955)
Times 13/9/40
Correspondence with and interviews by author.

CHAPTER 5

Balfour ....(1979)
Brown.............................(1998)
Brown.............................(1981)
Collier ....(1979)
Delmer ....(1962)
Ford.............................(1971)
Foynes ....(1994)
Glover ....(1990)
Graves ....(1943)
Howe ....(1982)
Schenk.............................(1990)
Shirer.............................(1941) (1960)
Thomson ....(1947)
West.............................(1983) (1992) (1998)
White.............................(1955)
PRO documents:
FO 898/1
FO 898/6
FO 898/70
Various newspaper and television reports.
The Booth memoir is held at the IWM.

CHAPTER 6

Churchill ....(1949)
Fleming ....(1957)
Gibson.............................(1946)
Moen ....(1941)
Shirer.............................(1941) (1960)
Spaight ....(1941)
Thomson ....(1947)
Waugh ....(1952)
Various newspaper and television reports.
Hansard Reports

CHAPTER 7

Hoyt ....(1987)
Johnson ....(1978) (1992)
Kent.............................(1988)
Kinsey ....(1981) (1983)

Morpurgo ....(1972)
Rose and the Arrow
Sutcliffe.........................(1972)
Thompson ....(1966)
Wheatley ....(1934)
White.............................(1948)
PRO documents:
HO 207/1175
WO 166/1038
Correspondence with and interviews by author.
Various newspaper and televison reports.

CHAPTER 8

Correspondence with and interviews by author.

BIBLIOGRAPHY

All titles published in London unless otherwise stated.

AGAR, Captain Augustus : Footprints in the Sea (Evans, 1959)

ANSEL, Walter : Hitler Confronts England (Duke University Press,USA 1960)

BALFOUR, Michael : Propaganda In War 1939-1945 (Routledge & Kegan Paul, 1979)

BANKS, Sir Donald : Flame Over Britain (Sampson Low Marston & Co, 1946)

Bomber Command-9/39 to 7/41 (HMSO, 1941)

BOWYER, Michael : 2 Group RAF-A Complete History (Faber, 1974)

BRADLEY, General Omar : A Soldier's Story (Rand McNally, New York, 1951)

BROOKS, Andrew : Photo Reconnaissance-The Operational History (Ian Allan, 1975)

BROWN, R Douglas : East Anglia 1939 (Terence Dalton, Lavenham,1981)

BROWN, R Douglas : East Anglia 1940 (Terence Dalton, Lavenham, 1981)

BROWN, Richard : Mr Brown's Diary (Sutton, Stroud, 1998)

CHURCHILL, Winston S : The Second World War Vol II-Their Finest Hour (Cassell, 1949)

COLLIER, Basil : The Defence of the United Kingdom (HMSO, 1957)

COLLIER, Richard : 1940-The World in Flames (Hamish Hamilton, 1979)

COLVILLE, John : The Fringes of Power (Hodder & Stoughton, 1985)

CRUICKSHANK, Dr C : The Fourth Arm-Psychological Warfare 1939-45 (Davis-Poynter, 1977)

DEACON, Richard : British Secret Service [Revised Edition] (Grafton, 1991)

DELMER, Sefton : Black Boomerang (Secker & Warburg, 1962)

DRAPER, Alfred : Operation Fish (Cassell, 1979)

FEUCHTER, Georg : Geschichte des Luftkriegs (Athenaum Verlag, Germany, 1954)

FLEMING Peter : Invasion, 1940 (Rupert Hart-Davis, 1957)

FORD, Corey : Donovan of OSS (Robert Hale, 1971)

FOYNES, Julian : The Battle of the East Coast 1939-45 (private printing, 1994)

GIBSON, Guy : Enemy Coast Ahead (Michael Joseph, 1946)

GLOVER, Michael : Invasion Scare 1940 (Leo Cooper, 1990)

GRAVES, Charles : The Home Guard of Britain (Hutchinson, 1943)

GRINNELL-MILNE, Duncan : The Silent Victory (Bodley Head, 1958)

HARRIS, Robert/PAXMAN, Jeremy : A Higher Form of Killing (Chatto & Windus, 1982)

HASTINGS, Max : Bomber Command (Michael Joseph, 1979)

HINSLEY, FH : British Intelligence in the Second World War (HMSO, 1979)

HOHNE, Heinz : Canaris (Weidenfeld & Nicholson, 1979)

HORNE, Alistair : To Lose a Battle-France 1940 (Macmillan, 1969)

HOWE, Ellic : The Black Game (Michael Joseph, 1982)

HOYT, Edwyn : The Invasion Before Normandy (Robert Hale, 1987)
Incendiary Weapons (SIPRI, Sweden, 1975)
HYDE, H Montgomery : Secret Intelligence Agent (Constable, 1982)
HYDE, H Montgomery : The Quiet Canadian (Hamish Hamilton, 1962)
IRONSIDE, Sir Edmund : The Ironside Diaries 1937-1940 (Constable, 1962)
JACKSON, Robert : Before the Storm-The Story of Bomber Command 1939-1942 (Arthur Barker, 1972)
JOHNSON, Derek : East Anglia At War 1939-1945 [First Edition] (Jarrold, Norwich, 1978)
JOHNSON, Derek : East Anglia At War 1939-1945 [Second Edition] (Jarrold, Norwich, 1992)
KENT, Peter : Fortifications of East Anglia (Terence Dalton, Lavenham, 1988)
KINSEY, Gordon : Bawdsey-Birth of the Beam (Terence Dalton, Lavenham, 1983)
KINSEY, Gordon : Orfordness-Secret Site (Terence Dalton, Lavenham, 1981)
KNIGHT, Dennis : Harvest of Messerschmitts (Wingham Press, 1990)
LAMPE, David : The Last Ditch (Cassell, 1968)
LECKIE, Robert : Delivered From Evil (Harper and Row, New York, 1987)
LONGMATE, Norman : How We Lived Then (Hutchinson, 1971)
LONGMATE, Norman : If Britain Had Fallen (BBC/Hutchinson, 1972)
LONGMATE, Norman : Island Fortress-The Defence of Great Britain 1603-1945 (Hutchinson, 1991)
MACBEAN, Wing Commander John/HOGBEN, Major Arthur : Bombs Gone (PSL, Wellingborough, 1990)
MACKSEY, Kenneth : Invasion-The German Invasion of England, July 1940 (Greenhill, 1980)
MANSTEIN, Field Marshal Erich von : Lost Victories (Methuen, 1958)
MARTIENSSEN, A : Hitler & His Admirals (Secker & Warburg, 1948)
MASTERMAN, JC : The Double-Cross System (Yale University Press, USA, 1972)
McKEE, Alexander : Strike From The Sky-The Battle of Britain Story (Souvenir Press, 1960)
MIDDLEBROOK, Martin/EVERITT, Chris : The Bomber Command War Diaries 1939-1945 (Viking, 1985)
MOEN, Lars : Under the Iron Heel (Robert Hale, 1941)
MORGAN, Sir Frederick : Overture to Overlord (Hodder & Stoughton, 1950)
MORPURGO, JE : Barnes Wallis (Longman, 1972)
MOYES, Philip : Bomber Squadrons of the RAF (McDonald, 1964)
PARTINGTON, JR : A History of Greek Fire and Gunpowder (Heffer, Cambridge, 1960)
PAWLE, Gerald : The Secret War (Harrap, 1956)
RAMSAY, Winston (ed) : The Blitz Then and Now (Vol 1) (After the Battle)
RAMSAY, Winston (ed) : The Blitz Then and Now (Vol 2) (After the Battle)
RICHARDS, Denis : Royal Air Force 1939-1945 Vol One-The Fight at Odds (HMSO, 1953)
ROBERTS, A/GUELFF, R (editors) : Documents on the Laws of War (Clarendon

Press, Oxford, 1989)

The Rose & The Arrow-A Life Story of the 136th Field Regiment Royal Artillery 1939-1946 (Private Printing)

ROSKILL, Stephen : Hankey-Man of Secrets Vol 1 (Collins, 1970)

ROSKILL, Stephen : Hankey-Man of Secrets Vol 3 (Collins, 1974)

ROSKILL, Stephen : The War at Sea Vol I (HMSO, 1954)

RUGE, Friedrich : Sea Warfare 1939-1945-A German Viewpoint (Cassell, 1957)

SCHENK, Peter : The Invasion of England 1940 (Conway Maritime Press, 1990)

SHIRER, William : Berlin Diary (Alfred Knopf, New York, 1941)

SHIRER, William : The Rise & Fall of the Third Reich (Secker & Warburg, 1960)

SMALL, Ken : The Forgotten Dead (Bloomsbury, 1988)

SMITH, R Harris : OSS-the Secret History of America's First CIA (University of California Press, USA, 1972)

SPAIGHT, JM : The Battle of Britain 1940 (Geoffrey Bles, 1941)

SPEER, Albert : Inside the Third Reich (Weidenfeld and Nicholson, 1970)

STEVENSON, William : A Man Called Intrepid (Macmillan, 1976)

SUTCLIFFE, Sheila : Martello Towers (David & Charles, 1972)

THOMAS, Andy : Effects of Chemical Warfare-a selective review and bibliography of British state papers (SIPRI, 1985)

THOMPSON, Laurence : 1940-Year of Legend, Year of History (Collins, 1966)

THOMSON, Rear-Admiral George : Blue Pencil Admiral (Sampson Low, Marston & Co, 1947)

WAUGH, Evelyn : Men at Arms (Chapman & Hall, 1952)

WEEKS, John : Men Against Tanks-A History of Anti-Tank Warfare (David & Charles, 1975)

WEST, Nigel : MI5-British Security Service Operations 1939-45 (The Bodley Head, 1981)

WEST, Nigel : MI6-British Secret Intelligence Service Operations 1939-45 (Weidenfeld & Nicolson, 1983)

WEST, Nigel : Unreliable Witness (Weidenfeld & Nicolson, 1984)

WEST, Nigel : Secret War-The Story of SOE (Hodder & Stoughton, 1992)

WEST, Nigel : British Security Co-ordination (St Ermins, 1998)

WHEATLEY, Dennis : Black August (Hutchinson, 1934)

WHEATLEY, Dennis : Stranger Than Fiction (Hutchinson, 1959)

WHEATLEY, Ronald : Operation Sealion (Oxford University Press, Oxford, 1958)

WHITE, Archie : Tideways & Byways in Essex & Suffolk (1948)

WHITE, John Baker : The Big Lie (Evans, 1955)

WINTERBOTHAM, FW : The Ultra Secret (Weidenfeld & Nicolson, 1974)

Acknowledgments

A particular debt of thanks is owed to the following: Christopher Elliott, Ronald Harris, Edwin Horlington, Hadrian Jeffs, Bernard Kimpton, Michael Lucock, Robin Prior, Winston G. Ramsey, Dr Peter Schenk, Dr LO Standaert, Nigel West.

Thanks are due to the following historians: Correlli Barnett, Michael Bowyer, David Collyer, R. Douglas Brown, FH Hinsley, Ian V Hogg, Robert Jackson, Gordon Kinsey, Norman Longmate, James Lucas, Wing Commander John MacBean, Roger Morgan, David Rolf, James Rusbridger; Norman Scarfe; Andy Thomas, Major TIJ Toler, Dennis Turner.

Thanks are due to the following media reporters: Lindsay Brooke (Anglia TV), Christy Campbell (Sunday Telegraph), Russell Cook (EADT), Henry Creagh (EADT), Jeremy Hands (Anglia TV), Lisa Hempel, (BBC TV), Malcolm Pheby (EADT), David Weisbloom (EADT).

All PRO material is Crown Copyright and is reproduced with the permission of the Controller of Her Majesty's Stationery Office. All quotes from newspaper and television sources are reprinted with the kind permission of the editors:
© The Telegraph plc, London 1940
© East Anglian Daily Times Co Limited, 1974, 1984, 1992
© Times Newspapers Ltd, 1940, 1944
© The New York Times Company, 1940

Thanks to the following museum staff: L Ball (Commonwealth War Graves Commission), Terry Charman (IWM), Commander PR Compton-Hall (RN Submarine Museum), PJV Elliott and C Richards (RAF Museum), ID Goode (Ministry of Defence Whitehall Library), E Harris (The Barnes Wallis Trust), Anita Hollier (BP Archive), Gunhild Muschenheim (Goethe Institute), Dr John Rhodes (Royal Engineers Museum), Angela Wootton (IWM).

And to the staff of: the Imperial War Museum, London, the Public Records Office, Kew, Colchester Public Library, The Newspaper Library, Hendon, Bundesarchiv, Koblenz; Centre de Recherches et d'Etudes Historiques de la Seconde Guerre Mondiale, Brussels, Plaistow Press Ltd, Barnwell's Printers

(Aylsham). Thanks also to Terry Burchell for his work on the illustrations.

Thanks also to the following writers and members of the public who took the time and trouble to contribute: Tom Abram, David Alexander, Stuart Bacon (Suffolk Underwater Studies Unit), Dr JH Bamberg, Terry Banham, Pat Barnes, K Bathwest, WA Birkbeck, Francoise Le Boulanger, Peter Brackley, Major JD Braisby (Royal Artillery Museum), Andrew Burk, John Rux Burton, Winifred and Frank Buxton, Jamie Cann MP, Bruce Carter, Richard Challis Nick Champion, Peter Constable, Len Cook, Percy Darvell, Frank Dickinson, Jack Driscoll, GH Evans, Chief Superintendent PA Gell (Suffolk Constabulary), EH Gommo, Daphne Machin Goodall, Nicholas Green, Mr Grout, Sidney Gurton, George ffoulkes, Hollis Fowler, William Hall, Olga Hardardottir (SIPRI), George Hearse, Beverley Hodgkinson, Regina Hoffman, JHD Hooper, Doris Howes, K van Isacker, KT Hudson, Kenneth Jarmin, Peg and Eric Johnson, Tobin Jones, Rudiger Koschnitzki (Deutsches Institut fur Filmkunde), EC Leslie, Peter Luther, RJ Mabb, Agnes Mann, Mrs Marilyn Miles, Christiane Maubant (Musees du Havre), DJ Maxted, Eric Missant, Julian Morel, Frank North, Percy Nunn, TH Pimble, Reg Pollintine, Mrs P Pulford, Herbert Reinecker, J Rhodes (Royal Engineers Museum) Christopher Richford, GW Robertson, CD Robinson, Mr Seed, Edward Sharpin, LR Sidwell, Bill & Joy Sparks, TEA Spong, JV Steward, Don Tate, Alberic De Tollenaere, Alfred Weidenmann, DV Wells, Pamela Wilby, AG Williams, Ron Winton.

The re-enactment photographs on the cover of this book were shot at Shingle Street on April 22nd 2001 by Terry Burchell. Many thanks to all the members of the Civil Defenders, Vickers Machine Gunners Society, Royal Norfolk Regiment Living History Group and CC41 involved. For further details on these groups please contact jnice@ltmpub.freeserve.co.uk

INDEX

117

119